Cruise Route

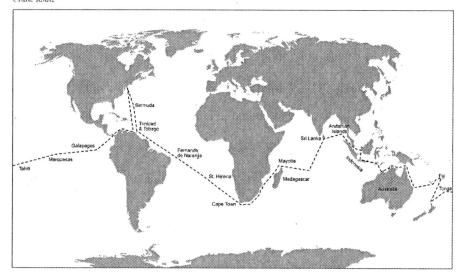

This Old Man and the Sea

This Old Man and the Sea

♦

How My Retirement Turned Into a Ten-Year Sail Around the World

Robert S. Ashton

iUniverse, Inc.
New York Lincoln Shanghai

This Old Man and the Sea
How My Retirement Turned Into a Ten-Year Sail Around the World

Copyright © 2006 by Robert S. Ashton

All rights reserved. No part of this book may be used or reproduced by any means, graphic, electronic, or mechanical, including photocopying, recording, taping or by any information storage retrieval system without the written permission of the publisher except in the case of brief quotations embodied in critical articles and reviews.

iUniverse books may be ordered through booksellers or by contacting:

iUniverse
2021 Pine Lake Road, Suite 100
Lincoln, NE 68512
www.iuniverse.com
1-800-Authors (1-800-288-4677)

ISBN-13: 978-0-595-38903-2 (pbk)
ISBN-13: 978-0-595-83470-9 (cloth)
ISBN-13: 978-0-595-83281-1 (ebk)
ISBN-10: 0-595-38903-1 (pbk)
ISBN-10: 0-595-83470-1 (cloth)
ISBN-10: 0-595-83281-4 (ebk)

Printed in the United States of America

Contents

Preface ix
Acknowledgments xi

Chapter 1	The Start 1
Chapter 2	Exploring the Eastern Caribbean 8
Chapter 3	Heading for Panama 15
Chapter 4	Crisis in the Panama Canal 21
Chapter 5	Into the Wide Pacific 25
Chapter 6	The Big Jump 30
Chapter 7	The Magnificent Marquesas 34
Chapter 8	Touching the Tuamotos 37
Chapter 9	Storied Tahiti and the Society Islands 40
Chapter 10	Weathering the Cook Islands 45
Chapter 11	Nuie and Its Caves 49
Chapter 12	Sailing and Diving Tonga 51
Chapter 13	The Battle for New Zealand 54
Chapter 14	Exploring New Zealand 58
Chapter 15	The Friendly Fiji Islands 64
Chapter 16	Vanuatu and on to Australia 74
Chapter 17	Roaming Australia 80

CHAPTER 18	On to Indonesia	93
CHAPTER 19	Meeting Orangutans in Kalimantan	98
CHAPTER 20	Singapore, the Malacca Straight, and Malaysia	101
CHAPTER 21	Exploring the Andaman Islands	107
CHAPTER 22	Sri Lanka—by Mistake	113
CHAPTER 23	Intermezzo in the Chagos	121
CHAPTER 24	The Island of Mayotte and the Race	128
CHAPTER 25	Madagascar and Its Villages	133
CHAPTER 26	South Africa and a Return to Civilization	139
CHAPTER 27	Touring Africa: Wildlife and People	148
CHAPTER 28	Going Home—at Last	156

Preface

I've sailed most of my life. At a summer camp, where sailing was a major activity, I'd been in a sailboat only a few times when the counselor directed me to take out a small scow by myself. I was 10, and I was terrified. I did it, though, and afterward, sailing crept into my life consistently. I sailed a Lightning, a Snipe, a Rhoads 19, and a Celebrity; this last, racing with a competitive crowd in Eastern Long Island. I saw a lot of sterns, then won a few trophies, and in those races, gained most of my sailing skills. In succeeding years, I vacationed by bareboat chartering, usually in the Caribbean.

There was only one answer for what to do in retirement. With the economy down and used-boat prices low, I was able to afford a better boat than I'd expected: a Nordic 40, designed by the well-known marine architect Robert Perry. The boat's only drawback was its name, *Gravy*; but bad luck or not, the name could be changed.

The idea of sailing across an ocean, even around the world, occurs to many people. Books, movies, and TV keep the concept fresh. Most people (sensibly) smile a minute and return to reality. They know they wouldn't like it. Their spouse wouldn't like it. They couldn't take that much time away from business or family or the golf course. They don't have enough money, they're too old, they'd get seasick.

For some, the barriers are insurmountable. Others buy a boat, gain experience (we hope), and push off. Now unforeseen problems appear. They don't like it. Even on a new boat, things break that they have to fix. A significant other who was a fine companion at home turns into something else under 24/7 pressure. I understand that in Hawaii, often the first stop on a long voyage, dozens of used boats are for sale. Reality separates most people from a major endeavor. Nevertheless, many complete big trips each year.

I write this book for those who seriously contemplate a voyage and for those who want a reason not to. I've included the ups and the downs, the agonies and the ecstasies—and the work. There is always something to clean, repair, adjust, or replace. Life at sea is not all cocktails at sunset, unless you have the budget for a cook and a mechanic. One acquaintance likened long-distance sailing to camping out inside a washing machine. That said, these were the best 10 years of my life.

I write this book also for friends and family who wondered what in the world I was doing all those years.

Acknowledgments

Nothing contributed to the success of my trip more than my phenomenal luck with crew. There were seventeen in all. I won't list them here because I've recognized them throughout the book, if inadequately. There are so many stories of sailors who picked up crew only to find them useless, alcoholics, thieves, or worse, that my luck seems incredible. A few were friends from home who were willing to brave airlines to find me and tolerate the vagaries of life on board. Friends I met along the way took as much chance on me as I did on them.

However this book is received, it has been improved by the editorial efforts of my cousin Dorry Ashton French. The quality of photos and maps is due to the aid, knowledge, and persistence of first, Robert Bushnell, and then Roswell Goris, who also taught me computer skills sufficient to handle the basics of MS Word. John Bean produced the beautiful cover. Finally, my brother, Dr. Francis Ashton, provided constant encouragement, both to keep going with the sailing and to carry through with the book.

1

The Start

I remember locking the door on my apartment. A simple one-bedroom on the seventh floor of a typical New York City high-rise, it had been my home for over 20 years. I was leaving all the security one associates with home and heading out on an adventure of unknowns. I was excited, eager, had no hesitation, but was also apprehensive. As I turned the key, I wondered when I would unlock this door again; when I would see this apartment again. Would I?

It was late October, 1992, and I had just retired after 36 years with the Procter & Gamble Company. Not ready for golf or gardening, I purchased a 1983 Nordic 40 sailboat—a 40-foot sloop designed by Robert Perry. Although I did not know this at the time, it would be my home for over 10 years.

As I lugged my last bags out to the waiting cab, I thought of the boat I had renamed *Chandelle*, after a maneuver in stunt flying. (Years ago I had flown private aircraft, mostly sailplanes.) *Chandelle* would be bobbing at the dock on City Island. Don Miller and Roger Wood would be there, having spent the night on board. Don, in his late fifties, had considerable sailing experience. Roger, although less experienced, was young, energetic, and owned his own boat. I had met them only briefly and liked them instantly. I was not to be disappointed.

The cab stopped to pick up Martha Waters. A Wellesley graduate and a New York lawyer, Martha was not happy with her career. She had approached me the year before and suggested that she quit her job and go sailing with me. She had been a good friend for about nine years and had sailed with me on several successful trips. We had always acknowledged that we were different personalities, and my initial reaction was that we would not get along well in the intensity of long-term sailing.

Over the next few weeks, I rethought her proposal. She was highly intelligent, dedicated to any task, reasonably strong physically, and seemed determined to tackle the intricacies of becoming a sailor. So I went back to her and said, in effect, "I'm game if you are." She was and set about making all the contribution she could. Having experienced *mal de mer* and determined to keep us fed at a level well above adequate, she tackled the cooking. A single New Yorker with a demanding job, she often made reservations instead of dinner, yet her culinary skills were excellent. Two days of intense work on her part had put 10 dinners in my home fridge.

As with most 40-foot sailboats, freezer capacity was limited. *Chandelle* had a large refrigerator but a freezer equal to one cubic foot. The problem was how to protect Martha's production. We started with the food well-frozen. We stacked it in *Chandelle*'s fridge, put a blanket on it, piled on 25 pounds of dry ice, and topped it with another blanket. The food kept solidly frozen for three weeks. Nevertheless, dry ice is extremely cold and would freeze the food to -250°F or colder. I was concerned that the cold might damage the fridge or the food itself. (Both pulled through.) Another possibility was suffocation from the CO_2 that dry ice becomes. However, after the initial cooling, that, too, became a minor concern. A sailboat is generally well-ventilated. All was well.

Martha and I had spent most of the summer cruising in Maine. Only one month remained for final preparation. The to-do list had occupied my mind for much of the summer and now seemed complete. The big items—life raft, safety gear, spare parts, repairs—were crossed off; although each time we crossed an item off, another appeared. Time moved faster than progress on the list, but when we walked down the dock, I felt reasonably ready.

I was to learn that you never cross all the items off. Initially, we would be at sea only four days, from New York down the East Coast to Norfolk, Virginia.

When we arrived at the boat, we were greeted with enthusiastic smiles from Don and Roger. I swallowed my apprehension. It was my boat. I was expected to know all about it, to have it in top shape, and to be able to handle any problems that came along. People's lives depended on it—on me—and I felt the responsibility. As events were to unfold, as I learned more and more about the boat and preparing for trips, I was never to lose that apprehension, that burden of responsibility. There was always the feeling of, What have I forgotten? What will break this time? Throwing the dock line or pulling the anchor is like jumping off the high board. You are never completely ready. You just have to do it.

Our time-pressure came from having to (and wanting to) join a group of boats that would soon brave the Gulf Stream and adjacent waters from Norfolk, Virginia, to the Caribbean. They were a safety net. Steve Black, a longtime professional sailor, would be shepherd. He would provide inspections, advice, and perhaps most important, constant weather forecasting for the fleet of 40 boats, many facing ocean sailing for the first time.

The Start

When we slipped the dock lines in City Island, the weather was perfect, the tide through New York harbor just right. The thrill of the bridges, the buildings, the monuments was enhanced by the easy slalom around ferries and freighters. The industrial world was in our faces, and from our perspective, appeared to be working flawlessly. We flew just one sail, the main, and motored because winds were light and the need for control was essential. During maximum tides, the eddies can send small boats in complete circles.

Passing under the Verrazano Bridge heralded the open ocean. Now clear of the land and most of the water traffic, we could take up our course down the coast. With enough wind to sail, we rolled out the jib and turned off the engine. Daylight provided visibility and security. The rush of wind taking the boat, the sound of water passing the hull (yes, I know it's the other way around) were as calming as the sound of a stream over rocks. It's these sensations that call a sailor out to sea.

As darkness set in, our world closed around us. The wide-open view during daylight now shrank to little beyond the boat's cockpit. The night was punctuated with occasional lights from shore or from other boats, but the distances were hard to determine. I set "Harvey," our autopilot (named after the six-foot invisible rabbit in the movie and play) to take over the steering. There is a challenge to steering in a race that rewards skill (sometimes); steering to a compass course hour after hour gets old fast.

Chandelle shortly after purchase

We were on our own now. The industrial world might as well have been a thousand miles away. The onset of motion at sea the first night out leaves little enthusiasm for a big dinner, so we snacked. Nevertheless, sea routine soon set in. With a crew of four, I set watches of two hours on, six hours off: comfortable.

Eventually, it was time for me to sleep. In my bunk the world became one of sounds. I tried to recognize each one. There was the gentle slap of a spinnaker halyard against the mast. It can be stopped at anchor by tying it off, but that's not practical underway. With a puff of wind, the wind-generator made a whirr that could be annoying without the knowledge that it was pumping electrons into the battery. Occasionally, I heard the chirp of Harvey's gears as he adjusted course. Nice to know he was on the task. Overall was the sound of water rushing past my ear—the sound of progress. I got up to investigate a "click" I didn't recognize. Finding a loose can or wine bottle, I stuffed something around it to hold it in place. That night, the motion was gentle and I could sleep.

Weather remained good, the crew worked well, nothing broke, and in four days the bridge into the Chesapeake Bay appeared right where the chart said it should be. We were soon tied up at the dock in Norfolk. So far, so good. Excellent, in fact, and I began to relax.

Sometime during the day, Don or Roger asked about our long-term plan. I realized then that Martha and I had never discussed it. Firmly in my mind was the thought of exploring the Caribbean. There's a lot of it, from the easternmost islands to Belize and Panama. That's what most yachties with time available do. I began to voice this thought when Martha interrupted me. "Don't you understand," she said, "we're sailing around the world!"

I don't know what my facial expression showed, but my emotional jaw dropped. I had not considered that. I also knew that she did not understand the implications. I said nothing at the time, but a few weeks later, said to her (in effect), "OK, I'm game, but you don't know as much as you think you do. We should spend a year in the Caribbean learning the boat, making modifications, learning more sailing."

My occasional contact with graduates of Seven Sister schools had taught me never to expect humility. So while I think she was taken aback by my questioning her ability, she agreed. Later, she told me that was one of my better decisions.

Our shepherd to the Caribbean, Steve Black, and his organization now took over with inspections and lectures. I was persuaded to do some upgrades and learn a few things about safety at sea. The weather did not cooperate. Instead, it turned nasty. With 40 boats on his hands, Steve postponed the start. Ultimately,

Steve's weather forecaster concluded that weather would be bad for a week or more—it was, after all, late October—and we might as well brave it.

Steve organized a modified racing start. My racing instincts encouraged me to take advantage of relaxed rules and we led the fleet out of the harbor, except for one 60-footer. We didn't count her. When I tried to be cute and guess what the winds would do, I guessed wrong. Well, it wasn't a real race, anyway. The other boats charged off to St. Thomas, where Steve promised a survival party. I chose to separate and head to Antigua, thus avoiding the upwind bashing the others found themselves committed to by heading to the Leeward Islands. We kept in touch by radio, and the day before I anticipated landfall, I announced on the daily contact that *Chandelle* had won that year's Norfolk-to-Antigua Race.

It was not an easy trip. The weather forecaster was right; there was plenty of bad weather around, which the Gulf Stream, because of its higher temperature, tended to accentuate. The Stream was right in our path. We had to cross it. About in the middle, as the boat's motion reached its peak, just traversing the cabin—"walking" from handhold to handhold—required ample upper-body strength. A big jolt picked up poor Martha at a most inconvenient time and threw her against a shelf. The shelf survived; two of Martha's ribs did not. She hurt. Strapped in a bunk, even breathing was hard for her. The weather, not the least sympathetic, continued to batter us. Assured through radio contact that there was nothing for Martha to do but take painkillers and rest, boat life went on. Fortunately, we had the luxury of Don and Roger. Instantly, three watches became the norm. Later, Martha complained that she received less sympathy than she deserved. She was probably right.

For the last few days of the trip, the weather provided fine trade-wind sailing. Martha was back on watch and enjoying accolades for her culinary skills. Our team worked well, and nothing major broke. That's how it's supposed to be. We began to experience the delights of life at sea: colorful sunrises and sunsets, light-blue water, puffy white clouds, flying fish and dolphins, and steady breezes. All demand poetry, but as my talents are otherwise, I'll resist.

Twelve days after the start at Norfolk, on the morning of November 3, the island of Antigua appeared on the horizon precisely where the chart said it should be. That builds one's confidence.

English Harbor in Antigua is surrounded on three sides by high rock walls. It has a narrow entrance and good anchoring depths. In short, it's spectacular. There are also services: rigging shops, sail lofts, electronics technicians, restaurants, and hotels. Many of the hotels are located in buildings from the days in the 1700s when the British—Lord Nelson in particular—ruled the area now called

Nelson Dock Yards. English Harbor is popular and crowded. We squeezed into a tight spot and dropped anchor. Only then did we relax.

The next day Don and Roger took a plane back to the real world of jobs and family. Martha and I, on our own now, went exploring. We sailed back north to Barbuda, then south to Guadeloupe, Isl. de Saints, Dominica, Martinique, St. Lucia, St. Vincent, Canouan, Tobago Keys, Grenada, and finally, Trinidad. All superb cruising: weather predictably tropical, brisk-but-steady breezes, lots of boats everywhere, and good harbors. We walked, took tours, and sampled restaurants. Life was great. We were getting this sailing thing down pretty well. (Yes, I'm skipping details.)

2

Exploring the Eastern Caribbean

Back home I was never one to get up earlier than necessary. Here, I loved pulling the hook at first light, first coffee departing the harbor, on course with sails set, Harvey (the autopilot) minding the course, and breakfast as we watched the sunrise. Leaving early means early arrival at the next harbor, which means having the best spot to anchor. If a boat anchors too close, you can tell them to move; if they hit you at night, it's their fault. Such is sailing etiquette.

We arrived at Trinidad and the Trinidad and Tobago Yacht Club in late February, in time for Carnival. The place goes bonkers. Were they to put the energy of Carnival into education, Trinidad might be the best-educated and perhaps wealthiest island in the world. Since they don't, it's great for tourism. Events include parades with incredible costumes. As I'm a bit of a music buff, my favorite event was the pan bands. These represent an industry (now sadly in decline) of turning steel drums into musical instruments and groups of as many as 125 into musical organizations. The competition among the bands at Carnival time is fierce, providing great entertainment at both rehearsals and concerts. Band members attacked and conquered incredibly complex rhythms with a precision on par with the violin section of a major symphony orchestra. Fascinated, I took a lesson. It's *hard*.

I realize I've not mentioned the third member of the crew, ship's cat, Spinnaker. I like animals, leaning more toward dogs than cats, but I like cats. Spinnaker, as a female Maine Coon—a hardy, intelligent breed—was as good a candidate for life on a boat as any. Martha made the choice, both to have a cat on board and to have that breed. OK, to keep a happy crew a captain will make compromises. Later, Martha would find comfort and intellectual stimulation in that furry feline when she perceived the captain to be short in these departments. I could see problems ahead. Each country had different immigration policies and any animal on board a yacht was a potential carrier of rabies and other pathogens. However, such complexities weren't immediately apparent, and by the time they were, attachment to Spinnaker (by Martha) overwhelmed any thought of change.

I mention Spinnaker now because a scene developed here that has long been etched in my mind. Spinnaker got sick. We were in Trinidad, and a local vet braved the bouncing dinghy to come out to the boat. He pronounced Spinnaker's problem to be associated with her being in heat and urged that she be neutered. That was OK with us, but Immigration would forbid her going ashore. Do it on the boat? Too confined, and the wake of a passing motorboat at a critical time might be lethal. What to do? The Yacht Club was built out over the water on pilings. Martha, being a lawyer, concluded that the second floor of the club would work because it was not "ashore." Club management agreed.

On the appointed day, the vet arrived with his anesthesiologist, a pole for an IV drip, and a pill for Spinnaker. The cat was in a heightened state of alert. Although sensing an unusual environment and that she was the center of whatever was about to happen, she was soon rendered docile by the pill. We cleaned months of dust off a card table, and the poor thing was spread-eagled on her back with a tiny mask over her face. She was out cold. Her tummy was shaved and then the operation began. Martha stifled a cry as the blade cut into the object of her affection. The vet pulled out a string of innards, said, "No, that's not it," pushed it all back in, pulled something else out that looked equally useless to me, said, "That's it," snipped it off, sewed up the incision, and the procedure was over.

Spinnaker came-to quickly and glanced at her bellyful of stitches. I figured she would soon scratch or damage them, but she ignored them completely. While her sickness did not return, later in the story, she will.

Trinidad was a great place for selective work on the boat. A local expert carpenter hired 17-year-olds and likely paid them little, but the result was good and at a price I could afford. The kids were learning a lot. *Chandelle* got new shelving, lockers, and additional storage. The tropical sun required more protection when we were at anchor. A shade to hang over the boom was the answer. One was easily made by a local shop.

The Yacht Club was a friendly, informal hangout. It had a tolerable restaurant and the inevitable bar. Not wanting that level of passivity, we listened instead to stories told on a neighbor boat of adventures up the Orinoco River in Brazil. The previous year, the river had been accessible through a narrow channel in the delta. Our friends showed pictures of monkeys, birds, and natives, whetting our appetite for more adventure. On *Tzimbe*, a South African boat, we found two young men, Keith and Rob, with a similar goal. More data-gathering, consisting mostly of conversations around the bar, determined that the channel to the Orinoco was iffy at best and that a great alternative was the San Juan River, due west in Venezuela.

Provisioned and with what charts we could find (there weren't many), our two-boat flotilla set off across the Gulf of Paria. We had to check in with Customs at the small and poor town of Guiria, where procedures were shortened (likely permitted) by presentation of a large bottle of rum. We were the third of three boats, and in each case the officials had to verify the quality of the contribution. By the time they left us, they were jovial and wobbly. We were none the worse, except for the loss of the rum.

After an easy sail down the coast to the San Juan River entrance, we dropped sail and began the trip upriver. Wide and deep, with jungle on both sides, the channel was well-marked so that it could be used by oil tankers to access a loading facility way upstream. The sun was lowering and motoring at night made no sense, so we looked for a spot to anchor. The only place seemed to be at the entrance to a small stream, where wash from the stream had formed a delta under water. With lingering daylight and leaving Keith in charge to guard both boats (what he would have done to deal with an emergency, I don't know), three of us drove a dinghy up the stream. After 100 yards or so, we cut the outboard and drifted or paddled. Soon the fauna recovered from our racket and jungle noises began: bugs, birds, and mystery sounds. We saw parrots first, then—by the hundreds—the incredible scarlet ibis. Then monkeys. Totally quiet, they hung in trees above the stream. Five of them watched us intently. They were far more interesting in this environment than in a zoo. They seemed to take umbrage at our presence in their backyard.

The next day, we continued up the San Juan and took a left turn into an area the chart called "uncharted." Our advisors back at the bar were right. A myriad of channels and islands formed a mangrove forest. Like exploring a cave, we turned right, then left, wandering away from where we knew the main San Juan River flowed. We recorded GPS waypoints like a string of beads or bread crumbs against getting lost. It was wilderness. At sundown we anchored in a channel about 50 yards wide. Good, solid, mud bottom. An eight- or nine-foot tide made the banks too muddy for us to go ashore, and anyway, the forest appeared too dense for exploring. That left as our evening entertainment watching the ibis and other birds feed on the creatures in the mud.

We wandered among the islets and passages for three or four days. The only signs of human life were occasional platforms we guessed were used by the local Indians for sleeping or fishing. No planes flew overhead; there were no highway sounds. Our diesels overwhelmed the natural noises during the day, but mornings and evenings were magical with the sounds of bugs and birds. Yes, some of the bugs considered us a meal, and sometimes successfully, but we were the interlopers and we could use lotions and screens. Of the birds, the scarlet ibis were my favorites. Many times as we motored through a channel, a hundred of these gorgeous creatures would explode from a tree, fly ahead to another tree, then explode from it as we came on. I dubbed their behavior "a flyby of ibi."

Up early one morning for biological reasons, I glanced out the porthole and through the thick fog saw three canoes of natives watching us intently. From a distance of 30 yards it was hard to read their expressions. Fear? Anger? Welcome? From the deck, our friendly waves encouraged their cautious approach, and they emerged out of the fog. Now we could see that their dugout canoes were big, had six to 10 people on board, and included the very young and very old. Their expressions suggested that they had seldom, if ever, seen the likes of our vessels. Communication stumbled due to language, but eventually one small child offered a bit of Spanish.

When I asked "¿Dónde está su casa?" he waved a hand toward the jungle. They were nomads, living in their canoes and using the scattered platforms such as we had seen. Shy, they appeared embarrassed when I gave them paper and pencils, the only gift I could think of at the time. Their dugout canoes spoke of a simple life, though their children looked healthy. One wonders how they fit into the complex history of the area.

Cautiously, our two-boat fleet wandered on, acutely aware that grounding at high tide could be catastrophic. On a 10-foot tide over a soft, mud bottom, the mast would become entangled in the trees that crowded the narrow passages. It was a nightmare to contemplate. We nearly grounded twice, coming within two feet of the bottom. Relief accompanied our arrival at the Cano Francis, a tributary of the San Juan River.

Now with more confidence than appropriate from this exploit, we continued upriver almost to the ship-loading facility. The banks showed only dense jungle, yet our charts showed a town, Caripito, up a nearby stream. With anchors well-dug-in (we hoped) and boat cabins locked, we jumped into one dinghy to explore the town. This town had nothing resembling a dock, so we scrambled up a muddy bank and tied the painter (the line on the dinghy bow) to a tree. In many places in the Caribbean, the dinghy would have been gone in a matter of minutes. Would it be different here? We had no choice but to hope so.

The town of Caripito would make a movie set for a South American Western. Twenty to 30 buildings or houses were covered with dust and in need of paint.

Everything seemed dusty, including the people. The town existed to supply labor for the oil-loading facility. The only paved road ran right down the middle for the occasional trucks. In the absence of trucks, peace was shattered by the cacophonous blare from a huge boom-box in front of—what else—a bar. How the setting can affect one's thirst! Beer went down with ease as we attempted conversation with locals in halting Spanish and English. Hunger soon replaced thirst, and the bar was the only restaurant. Overcooked chicken can be delicious when enhanced by the setting and the lack of alternatives.

Now it was pitch-dark. Our anxiety over dinghy and sailboats grew. The dinghy was fine; we just had to traverse a mud bank to launch it. More entertaining was going downstream by flashlight. We picked our way through branches and around bends and around pairs of eyes staring at us. Some of the eyes were far apart. Alligators. One chomp on our inflatable and we'd be in the water and someone's dinner.

Our luck held. We avoided becoming alligator food and the sailboats were fine. Now we needed another adventure. Not convinced that the Orinoco tributary was blocked, we decided to find out. We motored back down the San Juan and south to where the charts showed the general lay of the channel. With waypoints that another yacht had used successfully the prior year, we felt reasonably confident. By now it was late afternoon. A strong, 25-knot breeze accompanied an overcast sky. The water was shallow. We had only a few feet under the keel. Lining up the waypoints, we needed just two miles to reach shelter for the night. *Tzimbe* drew less than *Chandelle* so went ahead to lead the way. Suddenly *Chandelle* was aground. We called *Tzimbe* by radio. They were also aground.

We were at least a half-mile from any shore or shelter. The sun was setting, the breeze rising. It was not a good situation. We put anchors out to keep from being driven farther aground and chatted by radio. Tide information, sketchy at best, suggested a small rise over the next few hours. The wind was building, there were swells, and we began bumping off the bottom. Engines on, anchors up, bumping every few seconds, we reversed our paths. Never sure which was to be the last bump, we watched the numbers on the fathometer begin to increase. We were free. Sailing at night back to Guiria, we questioned our bravado.

Sadly, the team had to split. *Tzimbe* took Keith and Rob north, and *Chandelle* returned to Trinidad. I had ordered parts for the autopilot and a few other things. I used FedEx and DHL so much over the succeeding years, I should have invested in them. I invested in boat parts instead. We regaled our friends with talk of our exploits, rested, and with parts installed, began our trip back up the island chain.

Everything had been going well, and our confidence as sailors grew. The game of criticizing other sailors became irresistible. The bareboat charterers, of which I had been one, were the easiest targets, particularly their anchoring techniques. They dropped too close to others, didn't let out enough scope (length of anchor line), and fed our egos well.

We liked to show off. One of our favorite procedures was to weigh anchor under sail. Before I got a windlass, I had to pull the anchor by hand—or you might say, by back. When at anchor with a light-but-existent breeze, I could pull the anchor without help from the engine. Once we were off the bottom, Martha would put the helm hard over one way or the other, and as the boat drifted back and to the side, she would roll out the jib and sail silently through the fleet of anchored boats, while I stowed the anchor and rode. She had most of the fun, and I, most of the work, but it was jointly satisfying. Once beyond the anchored boats, we would bring *Chandelle* around to close-hauled on the jib. I would raise the mainsail and we would be underway. No mechanical help, just a touch of muscle, a bit of skill, and we could gloat.

Martha lost none of her enthusiasm for pushing off around the world, so I began to look at every item on the boat with a critical eye. The result included new batteries, a new alternator, a water-maker, a wind-generator, and all new standing-rigging. It wasn't easy on my bank account, but my confidence in the vessel grew. Chats with others contemplating the same goal suggested we were on the right track. These projects took us north to St. Martin and then back south to Carriocou, all in the period of March to July. Hurricane season was looming. We had to get south, all the way back to Trinidad.

Meanwhile, we had heard great things about the island of Tobago. It was hard to get to by small boat, but its relative isolation made it intriguing. With the reliable trade winds, the fact that *Chandelle* sailed unusually well to weather, and our reasonable skill at sail trim, we were able to fetch Tobago's north end with an overnight sail from Carriocou. Friends Bob and Louise Messner flew in to join us and *Chandelle* explored almost every harbor and village. The harbors were pretty, but roll-y, and occasionally seas rolled the boat enough to spill a glass of wine.

We attended a native event, billed as an "Old-Time Wedding," that was conducted in a church. A young couple pretended to go through the marriage ceremony. A humorist was planted in the congregation, and when the "preacher" said, "Do you take this fine woman…," we heard, "Fine woman, indeed. She's wanted for murder in the next town!"—followed by gales of laughter from the congregation. The "wedding" was followed by a festival, in all a native experience for us.

Back in Trinidad, the Messners departed, and we began seriously to contemplate the tasks ahead. Much information traveled up and down the dock and bar. We borrowed, traded, and photocopied charts. Yes, photocopied. The book says never to use photocopied charts, but when you consider that some will be used for only minutes, the cost makes a photocopy an attractive option.

We planned provisions. We read cruising guides. Finally, on October 11, 1994, we tossed the dock lines and headed west along the Venezuelan coast. It was a big step. Could we change our minds and return? Yes, but the farther we went, the harder that would be. For me, the real trip had started.

3

Heading for Panama

Cruising the coast of Venezuela is idyllic, if you are going west. The trade winds are constant and at your back. Islands large and small abound. The island of Margarita, a large one, had excellent, low-cost supermarkets. Small islands, such as the Aves de Barlovento, where no building is permitted, are bird sanctuaries.

This first leg was particularly satisfying. All my GPS units (three) had gone bad, and I had to use dead-reckoning (a discouraging term). However, we had good charts for this part of the trip, and all the islands appeared on schedule. Bonaire provided a poor anchorage and lots of mosquitoes, though it was interesting for its diving and snorkeling. Curaçao had a great anchorage, a dock, a restaurant complex, and cars for rent. The 15 boats in the harbor were mostly American, and because it was now late November, someone organized Thanksgiving. We had three turkeys, various other contributions, and a great stuffing by Martha. It was quite a feast.

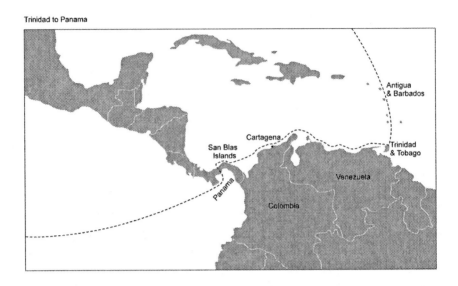

Trinidad to Panama

Roger Wood flew in to join us for the next leg. We were delighted to see him and just as delighted to see what he brought for a GPS, which we would want for the next leg. We were told that Aruba, the next island in the chain, offered mostly oil refineries and so was not of interest. Instead, our goal became Cartegena, Columbia, 300 miles down the coast. Getting there meant braving heavy weather and pirates. We were advised to stay 40 miles offshore, out of sight of land. The GPS would be invaluable, as would the extra crew of Roger. With the thought of pirates adding to the usual apprehension before a passage, we headed out.

Seventy-one hours later, after lots of wind but no pirates, we entered the harbor at Cartegena in good daylight. We had been urged to avoid running aground near the entrance because the locals had a reputation for coming to "help": help themselves to your wallet, clothes, food, and anything else they wanted. We made sure our navigation was precise. The trip had been blustery, but with all the wind behind us and little sail up, Harvey had handled the steering well. Since he was one of our most valuable crew members, we usually toasted him at the end of a successful passage.

Cartegena made a great stop. Word has it that the drug lords keep the crime low so they have a place to vacation. There is lots of history. The Old Town, with buildings 200 years old, is surrounded by a wall 500 years old. The wall was built by the Spanish to keep the gold they had stolen from the Incas or Aztecs from being stolen by the French or English. There were lots of battles, people died, gold and the town changed hands a few times. Has anything changed? It's great for tourism.

We stayed 10 days in Cartegena, touring, taking photos, having dinners ashore, making repairs (always repairs), provisioning. Everything takes longer to do on a boat, particularly when at anchor rather than tied to a dock. The weather was warm and dry, the days were pleasant, the nights cool. Our goal was to sail on. After a brief stop at an aquarium in the island group called Rosarios (how this aquarium supported itself was a mystery, there seemed to be so few visitors), we headed due west toward the coast of Panama. Thirty hours later we found an island in the Holandes group, part of the San Blas Islands, where the chart showed a good harbor. After a good night's sleep we were awakened by a gentle call. It was from a native in a small dugout canoe, a Mr. Robinson, who was camped at the island. He offered to be our guide. Although I'm often put off by such approaches, he seemed instantly likable and turned out to be a big help and an interesting man.

The San Blas are an archipelago of some roughly 200 islands near the Panama coast. The land mass nearest them has no road access, which has left the islands isolated and the natives, the Kuna Indians, primitive—until recently. Now planes land on a tiny airstrip on one island and bring mail, supplies, and occasionally tourists to a "resort," although the most informal one I have ever seen. Most of these islands are unspoiled and picture-perfect, with white sandy beaches backed by palm trees waving in the soft breeze. Storms are infrequent. The natives choose to crowd together on a very few of the islands, using the others to grow coconuts, a few vegetables, and fish on the local reefs.

San Blas Transport

Anyone with a small boat can wander freely, pick an island, anchor in the lee, and stay as long as supplies hold out. There were a number of boats doing just that: staying put for months to "write a novel" or do whatever else might justify apparent indolence and going to the Canal area periodically to stock up.

With Mr. Robinson's advice and guidance, we toured a village and the local graveyard. His wife had died a few weeks earlier and his description of their religious and spiritual beliefs enhanced the tour. One event stands out in my sailing-oriented mind. Mr. Robinson was 70 years old and obviously blind in one eye from a cataract. He had come on board with us for a few days as guide and navigator. We were on our way back to the island where he was camped, when I suddenly realized that it would be dark when we arrived. There were no navigational aids and nothing else to guide us into the tricky harbor. I said to him that I thought we should find a place to stop and wait for morning. He assured me he could get us in. I reminded him that my boat drew over six feet. "No problem," he said.

Heading for Panama 19

Kuna Indians

It was still light during this conversation, and I figured we would arrive in twilight. Wrong. In the tropics the sun goes straight down. It was pitch-black before we got there. Mr. Robinson poked his one eye ahead and looked confident. It was too late to do anything but trust him. He stood at the bow, pointing this way, then that. I was fully prepared to hit a reef. Suddenly, he turned and said, "Drop here." I could see nothing and I was a few years younger and had more eyes. The fathometer read 30 feet, a good anchoring depth, so down it went. With flashlight and dinghy we took Mr. Robinson ashore. The next day we found ourselves exactly in the middle of his harbor.

During his tour aboard, Mr. Robinson had complimented *Chandelle* on its sailing ability. With weak logic he assumed that I might also have a talent for yacht design. Next morning, we set about redesigning the local sailing canoes. They could go only downwind by sail, so did a lot of paddling. Someone had made a sketch for him showing a centerboard. I suggested leeboards as easier to make. I'd love to know whether they changed their design in any way.

Spending weeks, months, even years with these people would be fascinating, but their world was small. We had bigger ideas.

4

Crisis in the Panama Canal

Several places we visited were so enjoyable that leaving was hard to justify. Such were the San Blas Islands, and as I indicated, several boats lived there for months and years at a time. We wanted to see the world.

Next was the Panama Canal. The Caribbean entrance was only a two-day sail away. We made a stop en route at a hospital for wild animals on the island of Linton, but the Big Ditch was on our minds. We sailed in behind the breakwater with just enough information to get us to the Panama Canal Yacht Club. It's on a narrow waterway not easy to find on the chart. We joined the boats there by tying our bow to the shore and setting an anchor out the stern. While the club is nothing like those on Long Island Sound, it is a godsend. The house needed repair and painting, but had a bar and restaurant and staff with a font of information. We were told how to apply for transit, where to provision, and what we were in for. We were in for a lot.

Entering the Panama Canal

Once on the canal, each boat needs four line-handlers to manage the lines that hold the boat steady in the locks, a helmsperson, and an "advisor"—a canal employee with a hand-held radio who maintains contact with the canal operators. Like us, most small boats had only two people on board, so we took turns in the line-handling role. First we helped another boat, which provided great experience, then we asked someone else to help us. While our papers were being processed, we went through with a delightful young couple on their boat *Gone With the Wind*. It was a good trip with good company and gave us good information. Most boats take more than one day to make the crossing and spend a night anchored in Gatun Lake, which is at the highest elevation of the canal and is the source of all the water the canal uses. The hosts have to provide food and booze and the result is a good party. Once at the Pacific end, the extra line-handlers hitch or take a bus back.

On our return to *Chandelle*, we found that a storm had come through, our stern anchor had dragged, *Chandelle* had hit a neighbor boat, that boat blamed another boat and weren't speaking to the other boat, and cat Spinnaker was so traumatized by the experience she wouldn't speak to us for two days. Eventually we got everyone calmed down and began our final preparations.

Part of the experience at the Caribbean end of the canal was shopping in the city of Colón. I still think it was the most crime-ridden city of the trip, and there were worthy candidates later on. It would have been easy, but lethal, to walk to town. We always went by cab and usually with other yachties. Once in town, it was crowded enough to be safer. Still, we were usually followed by a disreputable-looking character waiting for an opportunity to snatch a purse or package. We carried little mace squirters, stayed alert, survived, and provisioned.

We had about two weeks before it was our turn to go through. After being inspected and measured, we signed documents absolving everyone of everything and paid the small fee of $250—minuscule considering the alternative of going around the Horn.

We gathered line-handlers from a Japanese boat, *Yu-U*, and a most attractive lady from a motorboat. It was a nice group, though made less so by the advisor assigned to us, Javier. He was a young kid who didn't speak English well and considered his talents too good to waste on a mere yacht. We were assigned to go through with a freighter, and when Javier saw it, he blanched. We thought in retrospect, that by the rules it was too big to be accompanied by a yacht, but we were given no option.

The whistles blew, the gate opened. First the freighter motored in, then *Chandelle*. Lines were tossed, gates were closed, and water rushed in. Lines strained at their cleats. Cleats held. First lock, OK.

Second lock, same procedure, but now we had wind from behind. Javier ordered the lines from shore dropped. (He, as an advisor, was not supposed to give orders.) Without lines, *Chandelle* had to move to be controlled, and we were getting close to the freighter. At the helm, Martha swerved to keep our distance, but the freighter was still underway and the huge prop was still turning. Consequently, we were slammed into the side of the canal by the prop wash—fortunately, bow first. It was a terrifying moment.

In a few seconds, I recognized that while we had sustained substantial damage, we were no longer in danger. Still, would this be the end of the trip? I was depressed. Nothing to do at the time but keep going. We passed through the third lock (we were now 85 feet higher than sea level) and out into Gatun Lake. Although our main anchor had been demolished in the canal, I had a good spare. Once that was down, I realized that the lake was beautiful and no one was injured. The canal sent out an inspector right away, and he and I agreed that things looked reparable. Life could go on. A good, stiff drink and the aroma of Martha's cooking helped a lot.

The Japanese are not teetotalers and our line-handlers were no exception. Their captain, Yo Shi, was amazing. With his girlfriend by his side (he had a wife and son back in Japan), he regaled us with his drinking and sexual exploits, and he expected me to stay up half the night polishing off several bottles of serious booze. I have a strong feeling that my relative conservatism proved a great disappointment to him. Eventually, we bedded down and I fell into a depressed, alcoholic sleep.

Next day, with a new and more likable advisor, we motored through the main part of the canal. It was awe-inspiring to see the vast quantities of earth moved to dig the canal, which was only one aspect of the trauma involved in creating it. Three locks down to the sea, with one or two mild crises, and we were in the Pacific. As we motored through a canal estuary to the Balboa Yacht Club, my thoughts veered from excitement at what lay ahead to apprehension at how to accomplish major repairs.

The Balboa Yacht Club was a huge, dilapidated, wooden building that housed a restaurant, a bar (of course), and a young man at an office window whose only job seemed to be answering questions from a constant stream of yachties. He and others were an enormous help. One lucky stroke was to hire Jim Lang, a New Zealander who worked as a boat mechanic. He and I worked out a schedule of events that would get us underway in a reasonable time. He spoke English as well as Spanish and found us a good welding shop. I spent as much on airfreight for an anchor and enough stainless steel to make a new bow-roller system as I did on local labor. Between hours of boat repair, we went into Panama City. Parts of it were modern and pleasant. Although it had its share of crime, it was nothing like Colón.

5

Into the Wide Pacific

After three weeks, the boat was back together and it was time to put to sea. As a test run, we took a two-hour sail to Taboga Island. We found out too late that it was largely a weekend place and that it was the weekend. (At sea one hardly notices.) We spent so much time trying to find a place to anchor, we didn't see much of the island.

Back to the yacht club for final checkout and provisioning. Now, provisioning was serious. We assumed, incorrectly, that there would be few resources once we left Panama and so had been buying everything even potentially useful. Still, as we found out later, what was available in various Pacific ports was far more expensive.

We had been collecting canned goods for a long time, particularly meat. Books are written on preparing for months at sea and I won't go into details here, except to say that we lowered *Chandelle* into the water four inches. Later, when I had the bottom repainted, I had the painter raise the waterline to match ocean provisioning. In New Zealand, over a year later, we were still using up food supplies, but better to have too much than too little. Standard advice for crossing an ocean is to have a three-month supply of emergency food. We overdid it.

It's an emotional moment when you cast the lines to go west from Panama. The chart shows a lot of water. We postponed the trauma by stopping at a group of islands called Las Perlas. Getting there was a slow, one-day sail, but with fuel tanks full and no chance to top off, we were determined to save all the fuel we could. We had no idea when we could get more. The Las Perlas Islands are aptly named. We stayed there two nights to get fully stowed and rested. Three other boats were there doing the same thing. Two were leaving when we were—*Melinda Lee* and *Rubiat*. On each was a family with two young children from six to 11. Since we were all about to tackle the same challenge, we became fast friends. It's easier to find the courage to pull the anchor if your neighbor is doing it. We left within minutes of each other and maintained either visual or radio contact for the whole trip to the Galapagos.

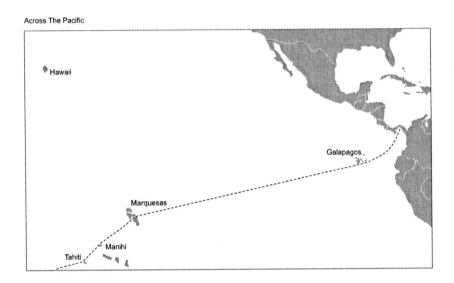

Across The Pacific

The Galapagos Islands were not far; we estimated, correctly, about a week. The challenge was the weather. The ITCZ (Inter-Tropical Convergence Zone) was operative. Meteorological details I will leave to others, but the result made everything variable: wind strength, wind direction, and rain. As soon as the sails were set for one condition, things changed. And the rain. "Tropical downpour" doesn't begin to describe it.

Much of the time there was too little wind to sail. Day after day we watched the level in the fuel tank drop. *Chandelle* was designed with an emphasis on racing. She had only a 50-gallon diesel tank, which would get about 200 miles. Not far enough. We stowed eight jerry cans all over the boat and strapped a big rubber container on deck. That more than doubled our capacity, but dumping diesel into the main tank at sea was a pain. After six-and-a-half days we were nearly out of fuel when we finally entered Academy Bay on the island of Santa Cruz in the Galapagos.

We were looking forward to this stop. The previous year, yachts were allowed only three days to visit. We had heard that rules had changed and we could get a week. We were not disappointed.

The harbor was not ideal. It faced close to the prevailing wind, was crowded, and required us to put out both a bow and a stern anchor to keep the bow toward the seas and away from other boats. Even though weather was generally light, we had some roll-y nights. The dock was inadequate even for the dinghy. We had to climb out onto a big concrete block and tie up to a piling. Bring the big boat to the dock? No way. Not even to refuel. To do that the skippers on the other two boats and I had to 1) rent a truck, 2) carry all our now-empty jerry cans ashore in our dinghies, 3) tie up the dinghies, 4) carry the jerry cans 30 yards to the truck, 5) ride in the truck to the only gas station on the island, 6) fill the jerry cans one at a time, 7) reverse the process, and 8) dump the cans. We had to do this three times, first to fill the tanks, then to stow the full cans. I was exhausted. Such are the delights of the cruising life.

Yet it is all worth it. Tourism is about the only thing happening in these islands and they know it. Everyone is friendly, including the harbormaster, who took $100 from us and promptly stuffed it in his pocket. No paperwork. The Customs/Immigration official took another $100, but gave me a receipt. A permit to tour the islands in one's own yacht is theoretically available, though so expensive that the only option is to take the local tour boat, which has the advantage of a guide.

Galapagos Turtle

We visited sea lion colonies, watched land and sea iguanas, saw penguins, and of course, the famous turtles. The Darwin Research Station has fine exhibits, including turtles you can feed. (Be sure to count your fingers afterward.) I suspect these huge beasts have roughly the same IQ as our common box turtle, but I felt as though I'd time-traveled to a prehistoric era.

We swam with a colony of sea lions that had grown accustomed to being visited. They seemed to welcome us and swam right up to within a couple of feet, turned to expose their bellies (a sign of trust?), then swam to the bottom as if to say, "Come into our world." It was a thrill.

With the families on *Melinda Lee* and *Rubiat,* we rented the same truck we'd used to refuel and used it to tour the main island. All day we watched finches, turtles, and other wildlife.

Swimming with Sea Lions

The week came to an end. After provisioning at a good market with local vegetables and fruit, we stowed all we could, until we were sure some of it would spoil before we ran out. (It did.) The next leg was the big one: 2,800 miles to the Marquesas. It was great to have the company of our other two boats when we pulled the anchor for that. We were all nervous, and the thought of company, if just by radio, was comforting. If someone were attacked by a whale, rescue was at least a possibility.

They were nice families. We liked them a lot. I'll never know how they mustered the energy to sail, cook, keep occasionally squabbling kids at bay, and keep them up with their lessons. Youth, I guess.

6

The Big Jump

Off we went: three tiny boats in a huge sea. Now *Chandelle*'s relatively high performance paid off. The other boats, both bigger at 47 feet, normally would have been faster, but day after day, as the sun came up, we could see our friends breaking the horizon somewhere. We could talk at will over VHF (short-range radio). We exchanged recipes for banana bread. I recited a poem. We compared watch systems. On *Chandelle* we did four-on, four-off all night, beginning whenever dinner was complete. We used our talents as we found them: Martha cooked, I washed up. The next morning, whoever had had the last watch had the whole morning off. Then we reversed it for the afternoon.

Mostly it was easy, broad-reach sailing. Winds tended to be light, so reefing was rare. *Chandelle* required two-person reefing, and we became skilled at it. There were squalls. It seemed that always at about 2:00 a.m., with good REM sleep going on, the cry, "Time to reef," would come down the companionway. At the same time, Spinnaker, on a 10-foot string to permit roaming while keeping her on board, would get tangled around a deck fitting and have to be rescued. Harvey, the autopilot, was an Alpha, and brilliant. We never had to steer. Many a watch would go by with no activity, not even a sail adjustment. Keeping awake was the challenge. Moonlit nights at sea and clear starry nights can be gorgeous. After you've seen a few, they all look alike. When it's overcast, spare me. Rain is worse.

Yes, there's hard work in all this. And that was the good part. We had two crises. One morning as I went on watch, I looked over the rig, as always, and saw that the port lower shroud tang was broken—not at the deck but under the spreader. The wind had been light, a moderate sea was running, and the sails had filled, emptied, filled, emptied, putting repeated shocks on the rig. What to do? The mast could break. Fortunately, I'd had installed a series of steps up the mast to that spreader. I dug heavy line and chain out of the locker, and climbing the mast a couple of times, rigged a line around the starboard spreader, in front of the mast, and down to the deck, putting a Spanish turnbuckle at the bottom. It worked. The rig held for 2,000 miles until we reached Tahiti, where we could have a replacement made for the tang.

That was the easier problem. Worse was when the galley began to smell of diesel fuel. Finding the source took days. What was leaking? Was it a fire hazard? Finally we saw a trickle from the sail locker next to the galley. One of the jerry cans had sprung a leak—not one of the six I had stored on deck, one of the three I had put in the locker. What a mess. We were a thousand miles from shore. We took everything out of the locker, put it all over the deck, rinsed it all off as well as conditions allowed, cleaned the locker, cleaned the galley, and put everything back in the locker smelling only slightly less, while all the while watching the boat. It was a nasty and exhausting day. Fortunately, the weather was light.

Our friends on *Rubiat* also had a fuel problem. Somehow, they had thrown a valve the wrong way and sent half their diesel into the bilge. Not only did the automatic bilge pump empty the bilge into the ocean, now they were seriously short of fuel, with half the distance still to go. Assuming reasonable winds, they could sail, but they needed the engine to charge the battery to support the refrigerator and freezer and to run the autopilot. Something had to be curtailed. With frozen food worth hundreds of dollars and no chance for replacement, they chose to shut off the autopilot and hand-steer—for 1,500 miles—with two small children too young to help, but able, I'm sure, to be small children. The parents' youth likely pulled them through.

Sailing is not for wimps. To keep up with the larger, faster boats, we flew our racing spinnaker whenever practical. It's a big help in a light breeze. Overconfident one day, I saw us closing on rival boats ahead. Hot for the chase and oblivious of wind strength, we were rewarded with a loud *bang* as the spinnaker disintegrated. *Shredded* is a better description. The wind had picked up more than I'd noticed. Martha tugged the ruined sail down and I set the smaller jib.

Martha with "The Catch of the Day"

It was not all horrible. Most days began with a colorful sunrise—a welcome reward for the night's watch—and brought many a fine breeze. Showers are natural in this part of the world and most were just a pleasing rinse. Fair-weather cumulus predominated and sunsets rivaled those in the Caribbean. There was surprisingly little wildlife. Dolphin and flying fish seemed to prefer being near shore. Two yellowfin tuna took our lures, and we took them for dinner. Meals came and went. Things broke and got fixed (generally). Night watches were long; day-watches were comfortable and often included a nap to catch up on sleep missed at night. At one point, a shout of joy came over the radio from the *Melinda Lee* because their GPS showed less than a thousand miles to go. That was progress. A friend on a boat we were to meet later confessed that he had read seven books on this passage (light stuff, I'm sure). I couldn't do that. There was always something to distract me. Our routine seemed perfectly sustainable, but when the Marquesas appeared on the horizon after 22 days, elation swept the crew like a shot of gin.

Winds were light, and in an effort to beat sundown, I turned on the iron jenny. I knew we were low on fuel in the tank (though we had plenty on deck), but I had reliable data on motoring hours per inch on the dipstick and calculated that we'd be fine. Wrong. Suddenly the diesel stopped. Dipping the tank (there was no gauge) showed it flat empty. What had happened? The tank had straight sides, which I'd inspected a hundred times, but the bottom was sloped—not obvious with the tank installed as it was. Because all I could measure was inches of fuel on the dipstick, my assumption of motoring-hours-per-inch was accurate for most of the tank but disastrous near the bottom.

We did have fuel in the rubber bladder lashed on the foredeck. As I engaged in the cumbersome process of hand-pumping out of the bladder into a jerry can and carrying the can down the rolling deck before emptying it into the main tank, the cook had words with the captain about skill-development.

7

The Magnificent Marquesas

Even without being the first sight of land in over three weeks, the Marquesas were spectacular. Young geologically, they are peaked and steep, yet covered with tropical jungle. With few inhabitants and little Western-style affluence, the islands looked all pristine wilderness. Our first stop was Baie Taahuku on the island of Hiva Oa, near the town of Atuona. Surrounded by lush hillsides, the harbor was perfect, with a narrow yet safe entrance and a concrete dock on one side. As we motored in the pass, we heard a shout from friends on *Rubiat*. They had arrived a few hours before. They held up a huge fish they had caught as they entered. It was at least four feet long and more than they could possibly eat. (Their freezer still held the food their hand-steering had protected.) They called on the radio to invite all boats in the harbor for a shore party. We anchored, cooked some rice to bring, and joined about 20 people from the other boats around the bonfire. Not only did we have a fine meal, we began to meet people who previously had been only radio acquaintances.

Commonly, in a major ocean crossing, there is a "net": a radio frequency and time during which anyone with a single sideband radio can join in. A particular net may exist for weeks, even months, after an arbitrary choice made by someone doing the trip early in the season is perpetuated by those coming on behind. The radios often carry for hundreds of miles and this is how much information is passed from boat to boat. Those in a harbor will give advice to those coming after, such as, "Watch the reef on your starboard side as you enter," or the location and perhaps the mood of Customs officials.

Approaching the Marquesas

We had been trading thoughts on weather and currents with 15 or 20 boats. Now we met the faces behind the voices. The camaraderie is unique. All have crossed the ocean. Something broke on every boat. Some caught fish, some didn't. Some loved it, some were glad it was over. A common thread for all boats was that the last few days of the trip had been agonizingly slow. We had heard about gooseneck barnacles; now we saw them. The bottom of *Chandelle* looked like a huge brush with three-inch bristles. In a good breeze, she barely made four knots.

After the shore party, I hit the bunk knowing that the anchor was finally down, but that days of scraping the hull loomed like a bad dream. Twelve hours of wonderful sleep and I was ready to join the battle. To my amazement, all the barnacles had fallen off. This unique species has no feeding tentacles, and instead, relies on water motion. With the boat at anchor, the barnacles starved.

Dinking ashore to the concrete dock, we anticipated a long walk to town to see Customs and the bank, where we needed to post a bond that we would ultimately leave the country. A good walk was welcome after so long at sea, but in a small parking lot by the dock were two teenage native girls with a pickup truck who offered us a ride. I was disappointed. Not for missing the walk, but because the girls wore T-shirts and blue jeans instead of grass skirts. Life has its letdowns. Still, the ride into town was welcome, the Customs people friendly, and the bank reasonably efficient. The town had mostly brick buildings that blended unobtrusively with the jungle. With friendly waves from all we passed, the possibility of crime, so ubiquitous in Panama, seemed remote.

We were now out of anything fresh and looked for groceries. Anything. Also, our fishing had resulted in more lures lost to fish than fish to us. The store owner seemed genuinely embarrassed that his prices for fishing gear were so high, but when I paid him willingly, he said something to a daughter who then brought us a huge bundle of fruit: bananas, bread fruit, and pompelmouse. He would not take any money for the fruit, and pompelmouse, a grapefruit, is now one of my lifetime culinary delights. We were going to enjoy the South Pacific.

After walks ashore to visit ancient stone carvings and the graves of Paul Gauguin and Jacques Brel, and after bouncing in a rented jeep over paths only loosely qualified as roads, we had pretty well done Hiva Oa. It was now mid-April and time to move on.

We sailed by day to the neighboring island of Tahuata, then made an early start the next morning to reach Oa Pou before nightfall. For something out of the way, we sailed next to Baie D'Hakahetau. In spite of the harbor being on the lee side of the island, the ocean swells came right in, making it too dangerous to go ashore. We thought we had been rewarded the next morning when an early peak out a porthole revealed native canoes sporting palm fronds all gathering in a circle with the young paddlers playing little pipes. Were we honored to witness a native ceremony? The sunrise? The proclamation of a new king? Then a small cruise ship appeared. It was all for tourists.

We felt vastly superior to the average tourist, so pulled anchor and went on to Nuka Hiva and Baie Taioa, also known as Daniel's Bay. It's perhaps my favorite bay in the world. It's almost impossible to see the entrance until about 500 feet away, yet the harbor inside is large, with good anchoring sand, high rock walls all around, a small beach, and a spring. It was a place that begged for an extended stay. We could not. After one night, we sailed on to Baie de Taiohae by the main town to get what provisions we could and to see the Immigration officials who would check us out of the area. Martha's daughter was to be married soon and months before we had had to choose a date and place from which Martha could return to the U.S. Tahiti was the choice. We had to get there.

The Marquesas exemplified the South Sea Island ideal: gorgeous, remote, many great harbors, attractive and friendly natives, and always one more thing to see. Paul Gauguin and Jacques Brel had chosen well. Now we regretted again the three weeks we had spent in Panama City fixing the canal damage. Martha's plane would leave Tahiti May 7. It was now April 26.

8

Touching the Tuamotos

The hundreds of islands of the Tuamotos dot the passage to Tahiti. We knew friends who had planned to and did spend weeks there, wandering among the many islands, some occupied, many not. Official U.S. and British Admiralty charts cover the area, but details for cruisers were confined to an informal little book called "Charley's Charts." Charley, whoever he was, had cruised the area extensively years before and had made little hand-sketches of most islands, showing entrances to lagoons, isolated rocks that he happened to know about (there were some he didn't know about), and good anchoring areas. Allowing for Murphy's Law, we figured we had time for one island and still arrive in Tahiti to meet Martha's plane comfortably. After poring over the dozens of alternatives, the island of Manihi seemed ideal: a well-protected lagoon, a narrow-but-deep entrance, no big hotels or towns to spoil the scene, and near our direct path.

It was a four-day trip with good sailing, though getting our bodies back into a sea routine was painful. On arrival off the entrance to the lagoon, a call on the VHF revealed that we had acquaintances anchored inside. "Don't try to come in now," they urged. "Tide is running out and too strong. You'd never make it."

Longing for an anchor on the bottom and a good rest, we had to meander by sail for four hours waiting for slack water. Finally motoring in, we discovered four sailboats on one shore near a small village. Assuming they knew best, we dropped nearby in spite of the carpet of coral I could see below in the bell-clear water. All boats got on the same radio channel and we compared notes on our trip there, on what to do there, and how long to stay. We confessed a yearning for a good snorkel but also that we were short on dinghy fuel. Instantly, folks we had never met volunteered to take us snorkeling the following day.

With a delicious night's sleep behind us, we happily climbed into their dinghy. They were an attractive couple. She was an American, he a Mexican Olympic sailor. They escorted us on one of the best snorkeling adventures of the trip. First, while the tide was running out of the harbor entrance, we drift-snorkeled.

That is, just inside the entrance, we jumped into the water, and hanging onto the dinghy, drifted out the pass. The current ran six knots or more, and predatory fish knew it could bring them food. Every color and size lurked behind outcroppings, including sharks. Big ones. I'd seen them before in the Caribbean, but none this big. It was little comfort knowing that most sharks will not attack a human; we watched them carefully as we drifted by. They looked well-fed and unlikely to pursue such an apparition as four swimmers and a large dinghy.

Once through the pass, on a plateau 10 feet down, we saw more colorful coral and more colorful fish. The plateau was 200 feet wide and a thousand or more feet long. Its outer edge dropped off vertically as far as we could see—100-200 feet. Here, scuba diving would be worth the hassle. Looking down through the darkening water, we could see that both coral and fish changed with the depth, but we could go no closer. The geology was also fascinating. Coral grows near the surface because the creatures that build it need the sun's energy. The volcano that formed these islands sank slowly into the earth's mantle at about the same rate that coral formed. As we looked down the plateau wall, we were looking back over thousands of years of coral growth.

After a few hours of even superb snorkeling, one gets water-soaked. It was time for another adventure. Our guides were planning to visit the local pearl farm, so we joined them. A tour to see the famous black pearls was easily arranged. The oysters had a pretty good life. All were hung in neat racks and food was easy. They just had to accept a tiny grain of sand in a critical place and grow a round pearl. That seemed fair. The tour included a shop offering pearl jewelry at a price that would not undercut shops on Fifth Avenue.

The local village was more modern than primitive. The French government had built a concrete dock and a short, paved street. The street was used by one villager to ride his motorcycle for about 30 seconds. (I'm not sure there was anywhere else for him to go with it.) The French had also arranged for a small ship to come by periodically. The ship hadn't been there for awhile, so the one or two shops had little to offer. We did fill a jerry can with gasoline for our dinghy.

Although more snorkeling beckoned, so did Martha's plane. We had to leave. Not so easy. A tug on the anchor chain showed us seriously snagged. I wanted more snorkeling anyway and into the water I went. Diving perhaps 20 feet, I could see the chain wrapped around several coral heads. With Martha at the helm and volunteers from another boat aboard *Chandelle*, I directed: "Move the bow over that way." "Now pull in chain." "Now that way." "More chain." We got off, and I climbed back on board after more of a workout than I wanted facing a three-day sail.

It was an easy trip until the last day. With my jury rig still holding up the mast, we welcomed light conditions, but on the final day a squall hit. The wind was no more than 30 knots, but it was the most we'd had since the repair. Would we lose the mast the last day before a permanent fix in the assumed sophistication of Tahiti? The seas built, the boat rocked, the temporary line strained. Reefing the sail reduced the strain from the wind, but now there was more rocking, which produced a shock load. With great relief we reached the lee of the island, and in the calm, motored into the harbor at Papeete.

9

Storied Tahiti and the Society Islands

Papeete. Civilization, I suppose. Car horns honked, trucks rumbled, a jet plane took off. To compensate, we had fresh food, restaurants, and ice cream. Anchoring required dropping an anchor off the stern, then tying a long line ashore so that *Chandelle* did not block any of two dozen other boats that might want to move. We spent a day there to check in with officialdom, then moved to another anchorage on the west side of the island. We heard later, after we'd moved, that a squall had come through, dragging anchors, damaging boats, and flaring tempers.

Tahiti being French and heavily subsidized, French was the language; English was barely tolerated. Still, Customs, Immigration, and banks eventually took care of us.

Papeete has an interesting history, but to us the town looked run-down and minor crime was common. At our new anchorage on the west side of the island by the Maeva Beach Hotel, life was simpler: one anchor, no lines ashore, just mind the weather. A dock by a dive shop welcomed dinghies from the several boats anchored there, and a fine supermarket a quarter-mile away completed our needs—mine, anyway. Martha was about to leave for a month. We sat down and made two lists. The first was boat-maintenance: things for me to do while she was away. This consisted of 25 or so items, including the mast shroud, of course. The second list itemized things for Martha to do: get daughter married, go to parties, relax, and see friends. Who said life was fair? My turn would come.

Martha left for affairs at home. I settled into the items on my list. (Spinnaker helped, of course.) I thought of the experiences in my life that had given me a measure of mechanical confidence. As a college student I had bought an old car, probably to impress the girls, but succeeded only in getting my hands dirty. (I won't comment on other successes.) The front-end fell apart, the transmission also, but I learned which end of a wrench to hold. A degree in mechanical engineering helped, but the ability to analyze the forces on a hypoid gear system was useless now (it always was). However, my Uncle Sam provided several months of training in electricity and radio communications as part of my ROTC commitment, and during the waning months of my 36 years with the Procter & Gamble Company, I bled the mechanics for their knowledge of motors and pumps. Other skippers had more skills than I, but some had far fewer. Some had more trouble than others with boats of comparable type and age. During the whole trip virtually everything on *Chandelle* broke at least once (except, thankfully, the mast). Still, there were skippers more plagued than I.

A hundred years ago Tahiti must have been a paradise. A large, biodiverse island, it is high enough to receive the rain necessary for lush hillsides and fertile valleys and is surrounded by the reefs that are so typical of the South Seas. Inside the reefs, the lagoon provides ideal anchoring for yachts today and in the past would have supported copious fish. Native historians told the early explorers that, yes, life was good. Periodically, however, testosterone persuaded the males to climb into their war canoes and go attack one of the other islands, usually Moorea, easily visible about 10 miles away. After the marauders killed a few enemy warriors and stole a few wives, things settled down, until the Mooreans came to Tahiti to do the same.

World War II transformed the Pacific Islands, Tahiti most of all. Today a jetport pours in tourists whose money generates high-rise hotels, high-rate restaurants, and traffic: civilization. Tahiti had a lot of what we needed—a place to rest, get mail, and get things fixed—yet for me, it was a waypoint, not a destination. I'm not aware of any significant beach, a likely disappointment for unsuspecting tourists. Martha used the jetport and I, the marine repair shops, so we were glad it was there.

On Martha's return, our projects complete, it was time to move on. After checkout with officials and an easy three-hour sail, we were in Cook's Bay, Moorea. What a contrast to Tahiti. The few buildings were modest. The hillsides were blanketed by forest, and behind them rose an impressive peak. We stayed two nights, toured the island, saw the dramatic view from a high lookout, and found a restaurant.

Next leg was an overnight to Huahini and the town of Fare. Chats with friends on the radio persuaded us to continue to Baie d'Avia, a large, open bay little touched by humans. During quiet days there I noticed a hill close by. Anticipating a great view from the top, I talked Martha into going ashore. From the beach, a road wandered toward and then past the hill, so I asked a native woman about a path to the top. "Oh, no," she said, "Bad spirits at the top. We never go there. No path." I was eager to confront the spirits for the sake of the view, but dense, thorny bushes persuaded me otherwise.

More radio chat convinced us to move on to Bora Bora to see a native dance contest. Each village had a team of 15 or so men and women who decked themselves out in full native costume and performed unique dance routines. This was not for tourists. This was far more interesting to me than a scrubbed routine for hotel guests. Some of the moves were highly suggestive, though we were told that things had been cleaned up from the old days. Missionary influence?

Sex in the South Pacific as the title for this book might have improved sales, but reviewers and friends, anticipating smut, would have been disappointed. However, while we roamed the area, we encountered native mores and customs that are worth passing on. First, homosexuality is accepted. I saw several instances where men exhibited the traits one associates with homosexuals. They made no attempt to hide their manner in public, and others were amused, rather than offended.

Based on need or convenience, children were often separated from their biological parents. For example, if parents wanted to go to New Zealand to work (many from each of the islands did), they might leave their children with anyone able to care for them. In some cases, most likely in small villages, if one family had many children, one or two might be transferred to a couple or family with fewer.

In some villages a young boy was assigned to be the plaything of the men. Volunteers were requested, but in the absence thereof, pressure was applied. The boy could opt out, if he found the requests not to his liking.

These descriptions in no way represent a serious investigation—perhaps *rumor* is a better word—but sources were multiple and from people who appeared knowledgeable.

To see the dancing at Bora Bora we had sailed past the islands of Raiatea and Tahaa. Not wanting to skip them, we sailed back east. This was a good decision. Their many coves and harbors, native villages, occasional resort, and easy weather all combined to provide ideal cruising—almost. Twice, the only anchorage was over 100 feet deep. At the time, I had only 70 feet of chain, which meant putting out 400 feet of rode (rope) to stay with the book ratio of five-to-one. It was easy enough to pay out, but it had to come back in by hand. Martha, at the wheel, provided encouragement, but my back signaled my brain to consider a windlass.

Late another day, with no good anchorage available, I dropped anchor near the edge of a reef, but in the coral. I hated to do it, knowing the damage that does, but there was no alternative. Anchor down, we were secure in the reef's lee, with a mile of deep water behind us and a stunning islet framing the setting sun. All seemed well.

The wind picked up in the night so slowly it wasn't noticed. An early morning peek outside showed us well off the reef. Sure enough, I went to the bow and found the anchor line straight down. We were drifting toward the islet. Fortunately, we had nearly a mile to go. I calmly pulled in the anchor, started the diesel, and well, What to do? There was no other place to anchor. Martha was up now and we proceeded to motor all day looking for safe haven. The charts lacked detail, so we used trial and error and a good fathometer. Eventually we found a mooring near a resort, just as the sun was setting. At the small, informal boatyard, I signed up for a bottom job (painting). My regular dives under the boat had revealed an increasing number of barnacles and other growths. These slowed the boat significantly.

Anchorage at Bora Bora

Another radio contact with friends persuaded us to return to Bora Bora and motor around to the other, or east, side of the island lagoon. We followed a tricky passage through reefs and shallow water and were rewarded with one of my favorite anchorages: clear water, nine feet deep, no tide to speak of, and perfect sand. I could relax. I could stand on the bow, follow the chain all the way to the anchor, and see the anchor dug in. A small islet, called a motu, shielded us from weather. The white sandy beach edged with palm trees and the dramatic peaks of the main island of Bora Bora were our backdrop for cocktails. Thirty feet to one side was anchored the yacht *Briar Patch* with good friends Becky and Bruce aboard.

The following day, we joined them to snorkel a patch of coral not more than 100 meters from our boats. There was a slight current running, so we dinghied upstream, and with engine off, drifted over the acres of coral below. All the colors of coral and fish were there. At one point, Bruce and I chased a three-foot octopus. He (or she) played hide-and-seek—running off to hide, only to peek out from behind a rock, then, as we approached, scooting off to hide again. It was another of the many days that will stick in my mind. Bora Bora was spectacular: the scenery, the quiet, the solitude, yet good friends nearby. We gave it four nights and longed for a month.

10

Weathering the Cook Islands

The world still beckoned. It was now the first of August and we had to be out of the cyclone belt by November. "Miles to go before...." We found a few fruits and veggies in the main town of Bora Bora and stowed and rested for a major leg to the Cook Islands. Crews on the several boats in the harbor compared notes on where to go. With many islands receiving good reports, it was a toss-up. We picked Raratonga, the southernmost, as did our friends on *Briar Patch*. Because theirs was the bigger boat and it's nice to have a close companion, I suggested they give us a two-hour head start so we could stay close longer. We left them in our wake. ("Doing a horizon job" is a more appropriate nautical expression.) We now had a clean bottom and were the fastest 40-footer in the area. Good for the ego.

Three days of broad-reach sailing brought us to the entrance of the only protected harbor in Raratonga, near the town of Avarua. Southeasterly trade winds still prevailed, although they were more variable now. We had to reef and unreef the sails. Later, in New Zealand, we had dinner with local sailors who bemoaned the need to tack constantly as they toured that country's coast. "Not us," we said. "We've been on port tack for three months."

On the way to Raratonga, one other event stands out in my memory. We had to pass close to, but not hit, a small island. I was on the night watch as we approached—very dark, no lights from any inhabitants—so I turned on the radar to confirm the island's location. It was two miles from its charted position. This was not surprising, since charts available to us frequently had printed on them, "Based on surveys done in 1890 [by one or another Navy official]." Charts showed the local relationships remarkably well because navigation techniques were up to that task. Longitude was the problem. Chronometers were good but not perfect, and eight seconds of time results in a two-mile error. It's astonishing that the surveyors did as well as they did. Since we were one of the first boats to leave Bora Bora, I relayed our finding to those following—part of the flow of information among the fraternity.

Here, too, the French had built a secure breakwater to form the harbor at Avarua. Heavy weather is common in this part of the Pacific and facilities had to support a sizable population. A narrow entrance and substantial tides meant we had to wait for slack water before going in. Once in, we found a crowded harbor and a delightful port captain. He was a retired freighter captain who had written a book on his experiences and who took great pleasure in cramming as many boats as possible into his domain. Two anchors off the bow and two or three lines off the stern—from each boat—resulted in a nearly solid web, with just enough room to allow the three or four local fishing boats to ply their trade. *Briar Patch* and two other yachts arrived after we did and thickened the web.

After expending all that effort, we wanted serious local touring. The weather turned nasty, but next day, along with the *Briar Patch* crew, we hiked across the island. It was a tough mountain trail, but the vigorous exercise was exhilarating. The following day, we rented a jeep and drove around the island. That didn't take long, so we drove around again. It was still early, so we drove up a mountain trail and blew a tire. We had to change it using an incomplete jack that we balanced on rocks in the mud. We laughed a lot.

Dancers, Raratonga, Cook Islands

Another day, we went to visit a radio ham named Arnold. He lived on the island and gave weather and other guidance to yachties (including us)—one of many around the world who provide contacts and information that for sailors is always comforting and frequently lifesaving. We made an appointment over the radio, and he welcomed us at the door of his modest home. To get to his radio "station," we wandered through rooms with beds unmade for weeks (by the looks of them) and a kitchen with a sink full of dirty dishes. His radio room was filled with tangled wires and black boxes, but he was superb at the job he had taken on. A professional weather forecaster we were to meet later said that because Arnold had been around so long, he was one of the best forecasters in the area. We made no comment on his housekeeping and made a small contribution to his budget for electric power.

A memorable event of our visit to Raratonga was the church service. Not for the religious philosophy, because the service was conducted in the local language, but for the singing. We had heard it extolled, and we were not disappointed. The islanders know they are famous for it and they show off. They are good. They sing on key, with good harmony, though with only one volume: loud. We forgave them that when the cleric invited all yachties to his house for tea. That was the only English used in the service, but it was all English at the party, with handshakes all around, many cakes and cookies, coffee, tea, and good conversation with the natives—probably local business leaders and officials. Toward the end, an official made a short, emphatic speech: "We are delighted to have you here. Spend money, then leave. Don't even consider living here. We don't want you." That was the message, anyway, and he conveyed it with a grin. We understood. They had a good thing going and didn't want it ruined by outsiders.

By the time we had done all the things there were to do, the weather cleared and Arnold announced over the radio that things should be good for our next leg, which was to the island of Nuie. Extricating *Chandelle* from the mesh of anchors and lines was a challenge, but all participants had had a good rest, so tempers were cool and cooperation ruled.

Underway again, all was fine for two days. Then at night the wind changed direction fast, from behind us to dead-ahead. I changed course to keep sailing, but soon the wind's rapid swing and building strength concerned me. Feeling wimpy, because one *can* sail into the wind, I put the engine on and doused sail. Then the wind hit at 40 knots. Overjoyed to have no sail, I called *Briar Patch* on the short-range radio and relayed our conditions. They thanked us and signed off, presumably to drop sail. They hadn't seen the squall, yet.

By next morning the wind had swung around behind us again, still blowing 40 knots. With only a little jib out, sailing was easy. The problem now was that two wave patterns existed. Where they crossed, they formed a column of water propelled by near gale-force winds. These columns looked like tree trunks. About 15 feet high, they leaned away from the wind, their steep surface coming right at us. Finally one hit. It forced the boat over on her beam, filled the cockpit with water, damaged the dodger and splash cloth, and bent the heavy metal holder for our spare anchor. The top companionway board was not in place (big mistake) and a lot of water went below. I was lucky not to be injured. Martha, below, was getting ready for her watch. She had no idea what had happened. Later, she said it sounded like glass shattering, followed by buckets of water coming down the companionway. I was able to watch the process. She could not. It was a frightening experience for her.

No more waves hit us, and after an hour or so, things calmed down. I called *Briar Patch* to see how they had fared. No response. No response all day. That was unusual and unsettling. Late in the day, at the time specified to talk to Arnold by long-range radio, we expressed our uneasiness about *Briar Patch* and his weather forecast. "Oh yes," he said, "a low has suddenly appeared right on top of you." We'd noticed. He registered our concerns for our fellow sailors, but was hesitant to call for search-and-rescue. The closest service was in New Zealand, many miles away.

Early the next day we pulled into the lee of Nuie, where a kind soul had placed five moorings—there being nothing but coral on the bottom. Shortly, we heard *Briar Patch* on the radio. They were fine and had a story to tell us.

Later, over beers ashore, they told their tale. They had tried to sail through the changing winds, but while tacking the jib, one jib sheet lost its stopper knot, flailed downwind, and wrapped around the headstay. Unwrapping it took over six hours. Bruce was on the foredeck, Becky was at the helm—leaving no one for radio contact. Although they knew of our developing concern, they had to solve their boat problem first. In retrospect, I was happy with my wimpy decision to douse sail, and I swore I would never let a stopper knot out of my jib sheets. (In three months, I would have exactly the same problem with exactly the same result.)

11

Nuie and Its Caves

Nuie was great. The only problem was getting ashore. Likely the same contractor who did so on the other islands built the big concrete dock here. It was substantial enough to handle a small freighter and would have been fine for dinghies were it not for the sea-surge endemic to the area. Also, steps to the dock at dinghy level were spawning grounds for a local poisonous water snake. Fifteen or 20 of them were right there.

We had our sea legs (tolerance for motion) from the passage, so we could easily accommodate motion at night on the mooring. For daytime, getting ashore became essential, and anyway, who's afraid of snakes? We could share the steps with snakes, but the dinghy had to come out. If we left it in the water, the surge would destroy it. The locals had built a small crane, and with the harness and much pushing and grunting, we deposited the dinghy on the dock. That was worth doing only once a day. Once ashore, we would stay. There was a lot to do.

First, there was the hotel. It was the only hotel and had been rebuilt after the original was destroyed in a hurricane three years earlier. We were shown a rock five feet in diameter that had been washed *up* a 50-foot cliff. Since the hotel was now new, I gave it three stars. The bar was almost always open and the hotel had a gimmick: the Nuie Yacht Club. Membership was selective; you had to have $20. For that you got a certificate, a wallet card, and a burgee. Reciprocity with other yacht clubs was minimal, but who cared? We all joined. Years before, someone had mentioned it in a magazine. With no residency requirements, applications came flooding in, giving the hotel a new source of revenue.

Nuie is the largest all-coral island in the world. Over the eons, weather riddled it with caves and tunnels. It's a spelunker's paradise. Guides, flashlights, and old clothes are essential, but thus equipped, miles of tunnels, "cathedrals," and squeeze-holes are accessible. At one point, accessibility for us meant diving under water to find a hole, then swimming through the hole into a pond on the other side. We all made it.

We had gotten word of a celebration nearby, and as we were walking down the road, a sporty BMW stopped to offer us a lift. The four of us squeezed in. Once inside, I remarked to the driver about the license plate: Nuie #1. He smiled and after a pause said, "Yes, this car is owned by the Premier." I smiled and looked him in the eye (I was in the front seat). After another pause, he smiled and said, "Yes, I'm the Premier." Our vision of a state dinner at his mansion did not materialize.

About 3,000 Nuieans live on the island. A greater number live and work in New Zealand. The money they send home is essential to the Nuiean economy, yet in a haircutting ceremony we attended, we saw an exhibit of affluence. At 12 or 13, boys get their first haircut. For this they sit all day in a large chair in their yard, facing a crowd of 50 to 75 neighbors (and a few tourists). The boy we saw looked bored and embarrassed—likely wishing he could just go play with his buddies. Periodically, someone came up and cut a sample of his hair as a keepsake.

Although the house was modest, the yard was mounded with fresh fish, local produce, and goat carcasses, all designated for neighbors who had presumably donated money for the event or for the boy's future. Refrigeration was scarce. Spoilage seemed inevitable and tragic, where means were so limited, but for us, the ceremony provided a colorful experience.

12

Sailing and Diving Tonga

The weather gods repented their former bad behavior and provided perfect conditions for our two-day trip to the Vava'u group at the north end of the Tonga archipelago. Arriving hours before dawn, we hove-to and were rewarded at sunrise by three whales breaching. One after the other, they rose up three-fourths out of the water and came crashing down. Was it a ceremony for the dawn? A greeting among friends? How fascinating to know. With good light we dropped sail and motored up a narrow tree-lined channel to the village of Niafu. As the sun rose, we could see the lush hillsides, the small houses, and both native and foreign boats. Tonga beckoned.

Tongans are known for having ferocious rugby teams for their small populations. Their Customs official illustrated part of the reason. He must have weighed well over 300 pounds, yet negotiated his way along the dock and to *Chandelle* as deftly as someone half his weight. Fortunately, he didn't have to come in our dinghy. The boat heeled 10° at his boarding, but he was charming and competent and he got the job done.

The dozen or more islands in the Vava'u group were as idyllic as any in the world. Nestled together, they provided shelter, many harbors, easy sailing, and good snorkeling. They were marred by bare-boat charter services, but I'm being selfish. The charter companies have developed charts for the area, which they make available at a small cost. Since the names of the Tongan harbors are unpronounceable, the charter companies call the harbors by number. A typical radio conversation between acquaintances might sound like this:

"Joe, we're in Thirteen. Where are you?"

"We're in Nine. Meet you in Eleven for lunch at 1:00?"

Tacky, but effective. Overall, this was one of my favorite sailing areas in the world.

Tonga is a poor country, though the people willingly support a royal family in high style. While we were there, one school did a fundraiser: native dances by the children for gifts and contributions from yachties. No child had shoes. The school was in need of every kind of supply. In the one town, domestic animals, such as chickens and pigs, roamed freely down the middle of the main street. Not surprisingly, an outbreak of typhus was underway. Periodically, natives organized a feast. We heard about one and joined 20 other yachties at the event. We sat on mats decorated with palm fronds and flowers and ate with our hands—fish, clams, pig, taro, and more. We could not identify the flavors, but the taste was delicious.

Bill Winters flew in from home, bringing with him a part for *Chandelle*. (I think it was a new thermostat for the diesel.) Almost anyone who joins a yacht in a distant land will be required to lug a needed part from home. We showed him around locally. Having spent almost two months in the comfort of the Vava'u group, Martha and I were eager to move on to the Ha'apai area farther south. Because it was poorly charted and visited by few yachties, Ha'apai held a fascination for us.

The water around Ha'apai was almost perfectly clear, which compensated for poor charting so long as someone at the bow called the location of the ubiquitous coral heads. Our rewards included some of the best snorkeling anywhere. Dive centers provide the only income for the area, but operate in a magnificent environment and should continue to do well.

By the time we arrived, I had a serious medical problem. Scrapes, perhaps from bumping into a coral head, were festering badly—particularly one big one on my leg. We had a standard antibiotic on board, and I was taking two a day. That was not helping. I seemed to have a systemic staph infection. On advice from a radio contact, we hunted down a small hospital on the island of Lifuka. A doctor (who was there sometimes) was credited with being a first-class dermatologist. Would he be there? As I walked down the dirt road toward the hospital, I realized that I was beginning to feel run-down, unwell. A small building appeared, and yes, the doctor was in. I sat in the waiting room with about 20 people, all natives, some of whom looked quite sick; others had babies. In a few minutes the doctor entered, saw me, and ushered me in. My guilt for crashing the line was overcome by his insistence.

He was one of those people who exude competence (others exude confidence, but that's different). I found out later that he had gone to medical school in Hawaii and returned to his homeland to do his best for his country. After looking at my sores, he asked what I had been doing for treatment.

"Two antibiotics a day," I told him.

"Go to three," he said, and apologized for having nothing in his hospital to help me. All he could do was have a bandage put on.

Walking back to the boat, I wished he had offered something more dramatic, but three pills a day did it. In three days, the healing process was evident. In six, I was well. What I'd had was life- or at least leg-threatening. I was lucky.

Bill's compatibility with heavy overnight sailing was limited, so he hopped a local plane to adventure elsewhere. *Chandelle*'s crew again played hide-and-seek with coral heads and enjoyed great snorkeling, which included watching apprehensively a six-foot hammerhead shark that looked to be asleep on the bottom, right next to the boat. We had to get by. We swam past quietly and he didn't budge. Perhaps he was dreaming of a lady hammerhead.

The weather was still docile, with only an occasional squall, but time was marching on. It was now late October and the cyclone season threatened. An overnight sail south brought us to Tongatapu, the largest Tongan island and the capital. Our timing was good. A major storm was forecast; then it arrived. Thankful for the small but well-protected harbor, we stretched our legs ashore more than had been possible for months.

Tongatapu had one ice cream shop and one traffic light and was proud of both. Martha's brother-in-law had been a roommate in high school of a member of the royal family, so we tried to make contact. We were told that the individual was living in Paris and would not return for months. The contrast between what appeared to be his lifestyle and the struggle for existence of the schools we saw on the outer islands was dramatic.

The appeal of the main town soon waned, and we succumbed to the temptation of an island tour. The tour guide did his best with the limited sights: flat landscape, a monument here, another there, and not much known about the island's history.

Both the forecasts and the weather continued to be bad. We used the time for walks, topping off provisions, stowing them, and resting for the trip to New Zealand. We knew the reputation of the sailing leg to New Zealand. We were nervous. We said nothing, but we were nervous.

13

The Battle for New Zealand

Never have I pulled the anchor for a trip of more than two days without apprehension. The waters on the way to New Zealand had a bad reputation, and we would be eight to 10 days at sea. This could be a rough passage. There were 14 boats anchored near us. All were getting regular weather forecasts, including one from a weather station in the harbor. Day after day the forecast was for terrible weather. As the season progressed, the weather got worse. Should we have left a month ago? Too late for that, but when the forecast said that a front would come through and provide at least a few days of good weather, 14 anchors came up on almost the same day and 14 boats headed south.

The forecast held for nearly three days. Sailing was good, and once we'd adjusted to night watches (always a frustration after several days in a harbor with regular sleeping hours), all went well. There was one crisis. In the middle of the night the jib halyard, which had been chafing at the masthead, parted, and the partially furled jib began sliding down the forestay. It looked like a tough fix in the middle of the ocean, but there was a good place for a repair right in our path: the Minerva Reef. The chart showed a ring of shallow water that would provide protection from heavy weather. Many boats had paused there in the past, and we had discussed it as a possible stop for its own interest. With daylight, though, the jib had slid far enough down the forestay for me to put a spare halyard on it. Crisis over. As we closed on Minerva, the weather was good and the boat was moving well. Better to keep going.

One morning a sail appeared on the horizon at first light. Whoever it was, it was a good excuse for a chat. It was the first boat of any sort we'd seen since leaving Tonga and turned out to be our good friends on *Melinda Lee*. Mike and I talked for half an hour—about weather, food, family, all sorts of things—until sailing needs called a halt. We were on slightly different courses to different ports in New Zealand.

The Battle for New Zealand   55

There was a ham radio operator in New Zealand who gave weather forecasts. Four days into the trip, the news was bad: heavy weather coming. We were warned, but had no place to hide. Hours later the wind began to build. Slowly at first, it built to 50 knots. Fortunately, it was blowing from right behind us. With sail down, except for a tiny staysail and a tinier jib, boat speed held at 7 knots. I thought of Robert Perry, the designer. He was my hero. The boat steered easily even with huge following seas 20 feet high. Rain and spray gave us minimal visibility during the day. At night we could see little beyond the cockpit. Then the autopilot, good ol' Harvey, died. He could handle the conditions; Harvey had been doing fine. He just stopped. With no way to troubleshoot, we had to hand-steer.

The skill involved in steering a boat in a big following sea comes with practice. The feel of the stern lifting as a wave overtakes it, combined with the sight of clouds and horizon, tells an experienced sailor what's coming and how to handle it. But at night—with no reference beyond the compass glowing in a world of black, with unpredictable and random motion—it is not easy. Martha couldn't do it. She did the last hours of the day so I could get some rest. As the sun went down, I settled in for a long night, a bottle of water and a candy bar for company.

It was easier than it might have been. With no sail to trim in the strong, gusty breeze, there was nothing to do but steer. That was fortunate because the helm needed constant attention. I couldn't leave for anything. Not anything. Occasional waves threw buckets of water into the cockpit. The water was managed, fortunately, by the substantially larger cockpit drains I had invested in years before, and the companionway boards kept most of the water from going below. It was a long, cold, wet night. I was glad to see first light and know that soon Martha could take the helm.

The wind held at 45-50 knots. Our visibility in foggy conditions was 100 yards, and we were closing fast on the rocky coast of New Zealand. Our charts were good and GPS was working. Plotting our position showed us five miles from islands off the coast. We couldn't see a thing, but five miles is well within radar range. A few minutes of fine-tuning the set, and there it was on the screen—*land*. Because of our experiences with charts being a mile or more in error, it was essential that we confirm the accuracy of our charts for New Zealand. They were close enough. According to plan, we left the islands to port and New Zealand to starboard and threaded a narrow path. Martha was at the helm; I was on radar, the chart, and GPS. Without any visual references to land, we managed to avoid disaster.

However, we were not yet safe. Eventually, GPS put us at the entrance to the river leading to Whangarai, our goal. Entering required a hard right turn—in the fog. "Trust your instruments," my flight instructor had said years ago, while I was taking lessons in instrument flying of private aircraft. Trusting my instruments required faith in technology. I was also aware that conditions were ripe for a rogue wave. A wave coming onshore can superimpose onto waves bouncing off a steep, rocky coast, creating a dangerous situation. With no alternative, turn we did, and after 100 yards, broke out of the fog. We could see for miles. Towering cliffs on each side bracketed the rolling countryside ahead, and the sky was blue for the first time in three days. Our survival seemed likely, or so we thought. There was more trouble in store.

Customs and Immigration directed us via radio to a cove, since we could not reach the inspection dock before nightfall. The cove turned out to be awash in huge seas. Although we'd been given an alternative, we'd had no chance to locate it on the chart. Then, with all sail down and the motor on, we were hit with a blast of air that must have approached 60 knots. The blast knocked *Chandelle* down 45°. A jib sheet lost its stopper knot, pulled out of the lead, and flailed downwind until it wrapped itself in a huge tangle around the forestay. (Just the problem our friends on *Briar Patch* had had on the way to Nuie.) A glance at the engine temperature showed we were overheating. Water wasn't pumping to cool the engine. We might have sailed, but there was no wind, except for the fierce gusts—down-blasts from the peeks around us—that produced winds from any direction. The jib sheet was fatally fouled, and it would take too long to raise the main. I tried frantically to free the jib, yet for the first time in several days I felt confident that we would be OK. If the motor quit and we were driven ashore, we were sheltered enough to swim to safety.

Suddenly the sound of the diesel changed. Water was pumping. Also, we were past the area producing the worst gusts. Running slowly to let the engine cool, we found the alternate anchorage on the chart and spotted it on shore. We wound our way through shallow water (after what we'd been through, running aground would have been tolerable, though exasperating) and reached the recommended cove.

With anchor down, engine off, and the boat somewhat tidied up, we looked around. The cove, the world, life—all were wonderful. In the waning light we looked out on lush, green hillsides. Trees, a few farmhouses, and grazing sheep completed the pastoral scene. What a contrast from a few hours earlier. The cove was safe and so picturesque that we would return several times over the coming months.

Looking up, we could see clouds roiling over the peaks we had just passed, confirming that the storm still raged at sea. Safe in the cove, *Chandelle* was now a level platform for the first time in eight days. The wind came to us in gentle puffs, providing welcome ventilation—more than welcome, since the boat and everything in it were soaked. Martha crafted a great meal, all the more enjoyable for our recent lack of food and sleep. Then, with bodies, clothing, bunks, and boat all wet, we followed the sun to bed.

14

Exploring New Zealand

The next day, crossing our fingers for the engine temperature (it held), we motored three hours upriver, admiring the green, rolling countryside as we went first to the Customs dock, then to the town marina. The marina would be home for far longer than we'd planned because of ship's mascot, Spinnaker. Having avoided many of the animal diseases, such as rabies, New Zealand had a firm quarantine requirement for domestic animals. Spinnaker had to be confined to the boat for six months with periodic inspections paid for by us. Weeks later, the rule was changed to confinement in an approved kennel ashore. I doubt that either Martha or the cat could have survived that emotionally. Actually, Spinnaker would have come through OK; Martha, I'm not so sure. Finally, we had to post a $1,000 bond. If the cat were found on land, the bond would be forfeited and the cat put down. No recourse. The captain pondered whether Spinnaker's good looks and delightful personality were worth it, but the question was resolved democratically. I was outvoted by Martha and (of course) the cat.

Tied to our assigned pilings, we settled in at the marina. At the time for the daily net, we tuned in to report our arrival and to find out how friends at sea were doing. We heard dreadful news. Forty boats made this trip and it was always a comfort that someone knew of our position as last reported. The *Melinda Lee* had failed to check in the day after we had talked to them and never did. The most likely reason was radio failure. Therefore, while New Zealand authorities had been notified, they waited until the estimated time of arrival before responding.

Then things began to happen. The weather cleared; a helicopter search began. Eventually the pilot spotted a person on an isolated beach. Rescued, she turned out to be the wife, Judy Sleaven. She had two broken vertebrae, a serious blow to the back of the head, and was critically dehydrated. At night, in the middle of the storm, the *Melinda Lee* and a small freighter collided. The collision destroyed the life raft, but not the dinghy. Only Judy survived. She clung to the overturned dinghy for over two days before being washed ashore.

This misfortune was a shock to everyone—especially to yachties and to those of us who knew them. They were two charming and energetic parents committed to giving their children a lifetime learning experience. Highly competent and experienced sailors, their boat was of hardy design and in fine condition. We had been about 30 miles away at the time of the collision and could attest to the bad visibility. They had radar, and presumably, so did the freighter, but to see on radar a vessel of any sort in those conditions requires constant attention and skill. Whether either was missing or the event was simply the result of consummate bad luck, I will let others decide, but like an auto wreck on the side of the road that slows all drivers, all of us in the yachting community knew that it could have been any one of us. We resolved to redouble our procedures for safety.

The collision, and Judy, became the major news story in New Zealand. Newspaper and TV coverage were ubiquitous; cameras and interviewers mobbed the marina. Within two hours of arriving at the hospital, Judy asked Martha for help. They had become good friends through their several contacts during the preceding months.

Judy was inundated with attention. Mail and telegrams poured into the hospital. Psychiatrists and church people offered help. Weakened physically and distraught psychologically, Judy couldn't deal with it all. Martha scheduled visitors, answered mail, wrote press releases, and perhaps most important, provided company and counseling.

Over time, Judy told us her story. She was on watch and fully dressed. She left the cockpit to make a log entry at about 2:00 a.m., and at that instant the collision occurred. Parents and daughter made it on deck. Son, Ben, in a bunk on the side of impact, likely died instantly. With the life raft destroyed, they were able to release the dinghy from its place on deck and cling to it in the stormy water as the *Melinda Lee* sank. The ship's operators, apparently thinking they had hit something, took a slow turn, saw nothing, and left on their way. Dressed only in night clothes, the daughter and Mike were soon overcome by hypothermia. They let go of the dinghy and drifted away. Judy, fully dressed, was determined to hang on—and did for the two days it took to be washed up on a beach. With her two broken vertebrae, she could not walk. From the blow to her head, she could not remember faces. Voices yes, faces no. She would not have survived much longer.

All of New Zealand rallied to Judy's aid. She had support from family, friends, psychiatry, religion, and most of all, her own mental and physical hardiness, which I witnessed many times. At my last contact with her, many years ago, she was well on her way to another full life. My understanding is that she found major contact with family and friends in the States too traumatic, and so made a life in New Zealand, including marriage to a New Zealander. I and the whole yachting community wish her the very best.

As a place to stay, Whangarai was perfect. We were in a small body of water—actually a river—tied to substantial pilings. Storms made going to shore in the dinghy a bit nasty, but hardly bothered us on *Chandelle*. The marina manager was a delight. He was an ex-yachtie and ex-national rugby player now ranked in squash for players over 40, and he went out of his way to be accommodating. Three large supermarkets vied for our business. Our arrival coincided with the end of fresh asparagus but the beginning of the strawberry season. A chandlery charged reasonable fees for marine goods, and shops of all sorts happily made whatever repairs we needed. From yachties who had been there awhile, we heard glowing reports of New Zealand. We were eager to go exploring.

The *Melinda Lee*'s fate made Martha wary of offshore sailing. Although I knew I would want to go to sea again, when Martha suggested staying in the country beyond the next sailing season, I agreed. That meant staying about a year and a half. The many shore activities, such as skiing, hiking, and just visiting another culture, made the decision easy. The cat would be under quarantine for six months, limiting our travel for the time being, so I joined a hiking club, a squash club, a choral society, and in anticipation of travel eventually, bought a 1984 Honda Civic.

I took several local walks with the hiking club, and they invited me on a two-week, serious mountain jaunt in the South Island, which was both kind and flattering. It turned out that my own hiking plans with friends from home conflicted—fortunately. Later, on a mountain slope, I ran into club members and could see in an instant that their youth (likely an average age of 40) and condition far exceeded mine. (I was 67.)

The squash club, too, was less than successful. Club members all played regularly; all were younger than I. I hadn't played in years and couldn't find the ball. I had one match with a 12-year-old girl and another with a 10-year-old boy. My ego wouldn't let me continue at that level, and my game was not quickly coming back.

Singing was more successful. My modest vocal talents were tolerated by the local choral society (no formal tryout was required), and they were just beginning rehearsal for a performance of "The Dream of Geronticus," by Edward Elgar. It was tough music and complicated, but they had an excellent conductor who also rehearsed the complete, although amateur, orchestra. Despite wrong notes from the French horn, the performance went well. Everyone had a good time, and the review in the local paper was kind.

While I was thus entertaining myself, Martha got out her green thumb. Eventually, her potted plants crowded *Chandelle*'s deck, and vines competed for space on shrouds and stays. The local paper wanted an interview. Martha agreed, with the proviso that the article mention our desire for a house to sit. The article appeared on the front page. Soon a couple came by and offered us their house for two months, at just the time I wanted the boat "on the hard" (on shore for repairs). I didn't relish living aboard in winter. All went well, except for the couple's expectation that the green thumb that had decorated the boat would now tend their garden. Instead, Martha took it to the States for two months, while Spinnaker and I, better at grease than greens, pulled wires instead of weeds. Still, most of the plants survived.

New Zealand has the highest ratio of boats to people of any country in the world. New Zealanders are excellent mechanics, and labor rates are well below those in the States. My elderly back was rebelling at pulling the anchor and tired of filling and dumping a deck-load of jerry cans. *Chandelle* needed a fresh coat of bottom paint, and the head (toilet) had a host of problems. Had the owners of the local yard known how much work I would bring them, they would have welcomed me with a brass band. By the time *Chandelle* splashed, we had an anchor windlass, a new head, a water tank converted to a fuel tank, and many other items done well and at a price I could handle.

However, low-cost repairs are not the only reason to linger in New Zealand. Per square mile it's one of the prettiest countries in the world. Flowers adorn every house, and gardening is a big industry. North Island has green, rolling farmland, countryside, and lots of sheep. South Island has mountains, desert, wildlife, great hiking trails, and lots of sheep. Martha and I explored by Honda. Jon Stoddard and Pat Collins flew in from the States, and we explored by rental car and foot. With full pack, we hiked the famous Milford and Routeburn tracks, as well as other areas. Hiking is important to New Zealand tourism. The government invests heavily in huts, trails, and other facilities with excellent results.

One of the gems for tourists is the farm stay: a bed-and-breakfast on a farm. The stay includes a tour of the farm—or sheep station as the big ones are called. We visited one that spread across 30,000 acres and were assured there were bigger ones. While we were there, we observed a sheep-shearing operation. The shearer grabbed the poor thing by its legs, held it upside down between his legs, and ran an electric razor over it, trying to get maximum wool with minimum blood. The animal was unenthusiastic. I was offered a chance to try my hand at it. My back sore from a long day in the car, I declined, thereby avoiding embarrassment for me and unnecessary suffering for the sheep, even though I envisioned the beast wriggling out of my amateur grasp and bolting for freedom.

With our visa about to expire as we approached the end of our year-and-a-half stay, my readiness for sailing the world's oceans grew. Martha's waned. The trauma of the big wave and the knockdown near Nuie, the difficulties on the approach to New Zealand, and the tragedy of the *Melinda Lee* weighed heavily on her. In addition, word came that a grandchild was on the way. Crossing oceans in small boats is not for everyone. She had given it her best. It was time for something else.

I had anticipated the likelihood of Martha's departure—she would take Spinnaker—and had talked to friend Pat Collins during a trip to the States, my first in two and a half years. Being the adventurous soul that he is, Pat volunteered for six months of crew duty, including the hiking mentioned above. More than hiking was ahead for him on *Chandelle*.

The same body of water that had caused so many traumas on our passage to New Zealand now lay on the path to our next goal, the Fiji Islands. Since Pat did not have Martha's experience, I considered a third crew member. We would have easier watches, and with back-up in case of injury or sickness, improved safety. At the last rehearsal of the choral society, I mentioned to another member I had grown to like, Robert Webb, my need for crew. He turned to me and said, "How 'bout me?"

As sailing plans developed, Robert and his wife, Idabelle, along with Pat, became warm and indispensable friends. I'm no cook and Martha's absence required a solution. I approached Idabelle, whose enthusiasm for the sailing itself was zero, and asked if she knew a caterer to prepare frozen foods for us. Of course, she had to volunteer. This was the perfect solution, and in spite of my outwardly strenuous protestations, she produced 10 excellent frozen dinners. Those and cans of beans for emergency would get us to Fiji.

Warmer weather heralded the beginning of sailing season, and *Chandelle* wended her way back up the coast to the Bay of Islands for final provisioning. Three days before our planned departure and two days before I was to sell the car, we all piled into the old, red Honda with the two dear friends from the vessel *Briar Patch* to go shopping. On our return, with car and laps overloaded and going up a hill, the engine overheated, blew the head gasket, and warped the head. Instantly, a $2,000 car was a $200 car. Cruising can be expensive.

Finally, we were ready. The boat was fully stocked; the frozen food in the fridge was packed in dry ice to keep it frozen. (That had worked perfectly when leaving New York at the beginning of the cruise.) All we needed was a good weather forecast.

Locally, it was stormy. We listened on the radio to boats that had left a few days before getting thrashed in 40-knot winds. We were glad we weren't at sea, but the forecast was for continued bad weather. Protecting our supplies, particularly the frozen dinners, required finding a local freezer. A restaurant let us use its walk-in freezer. As compensation, we had a farewell dinner there for 10 people.

A week later, the forecast improved. We borrowed a car to replace the fruits and veggies we'd eaten, retrieved our frozen dinners, packed them with more dry ice, and were once again ready to go.

With the inevitable apprehension at casting off the lines, Pat, Robert, and I headed north on an unsettled sea. Robert, an inveterate fisherman, hauled in a nice one the first day. We three looked at each other. No one was hungry. We put it back.

The first few days were blustery. The next few days were blustery. The whole trip was blustery, but the wind was on the beam or behind. We had lots of motion and were profoundly grateful for Idabelle's frozen dinners. We made the harbor at Suva in six days. GPS got us to the harbor entrance at 2:00 a.m. Preferring not to enter unfamiliar harbors at night, I contemplated waiting for dawn. However, a boat we'd chatted with over the radio had just entered and said, "It's easy." Ha! Still, a night at anchor was an alluring prospect. I, for one, was tired. GPS was not reliable for entering harbors (actually, GPS was reliable; the charts were not), but I spotted two green lights on shore that I hoped were lead lights (lights arranged so that by keeping them in line, a pilot can navigate a narrow channel). We entered cautiously. They *were* lead lights. We made it safely. Soon, anchor down, we all tucked in for a great night's sleep.

15

The Friendly Fiji Islands

All the way across the Pacific I had heard how friendly the Fiji Islanders were. After Panama, everyone we met on shore had a big smile and crime seemed a non-issue. With the possible exception of large towns and cities, such as Papeete, where crime and money-chasing were rampant, the natives were friendly everywhere. Why should Fiji Islanders be different? They were.

Robert Webb had to leave us shortly after we arrived, so that he and Idabelle could continue their trip to Canada, her original home. In Suva, Fiji's main town, Pat and I adjusted to the availability of ice cream, movies, and restaurants. We also took in a rugby match. We might have succumbed to total indolence, save for a few boat repairs. Harvey, the autopilot, had died again, due to a faulty drive-motor. I had wisely bought a spare, making Harvey's problem an easy fix. Not so easy was the leak in the water-maker. I plugged it with epoxy. Since the water-maker operated at 800 pounds pressure, the epoxy held for two seconds. That meant I had to order a new part from the States. Several other items also required attention.

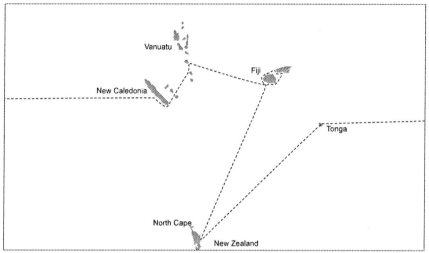

Through Fiji and Vanuatu

The part for the water-maker wouldn't arrive for at least two weeks, so looking for adventure, Pat and I sailed to the Kadavu Islands about 30 miles south. The Kadavu trip was an ideal introduction to Fiji. Not willing to trust either my luck with night entries into unfamiliar harbors or the accuracy of Fiji charts, I elected a 4:00 a.m. start from Suva. That was overly cautious. At 2:30 p.m., we were at the entrance to the main harbor on the island of Ono. We anchored near two other yachts and proceeded with the introduction process we had learned about. Much advice about what to do and what not to do comes from other yachties—at the dock, at the bar, over the radio—and where they existed, from guidebooks. As a result, we had purchased some kava while we were in Suva. The kava plant is a bush. The natives dry it, grind it, soak it in water, and drink it. It is the traditional gift one makes to a village on arrival, whether by land or by boat, much as we at home might bring a bottle of wine to a dinner party.

On arrival at a village, tradition requires that you seek the chief. One should be properly dressed: long pants, no dark glasses, no hat, and no backpack. You present the kava not to the chief's hands, that would be an insult, but by putting it on the ground in front of him. If he sits, you sit. If he picks up your offering, that is a welcome. (We never heard of a chief not welcoming a yachtie.) The chief or other dignitary talks in the native language (apparently asking the spirits for your well-being, that the sharks not attack you, the weather be good, etc.). If the chief likes you and has no conflict with other activities, he is likely to invite you to drink kava "with the boys" later in the day. Pat and I were so honored.

Before leaving the boat for this new adventure, we checked ourselves against the list of *dos* and *don'ts*: long pants, no dark glasses, no hat, no backpack. We rowed ashore and found the hut designated as the kava bar, although it was probably used for other events as well. With shoes removed, we entered. Once our eyes adjusted to the dim light, we saw a dirt floor covered with grass mats. Four men, probably in their 50s or 60s, were sitting around a bowl. The room was bare otherwise, the only light coming from the door and one window. The bowl was perhaps two-and-a-half feet in diameter and contained a light-brown liquid. As our eyes became further accustomed to the dimness, we saw what appeared to be a sock (clean?) soaking in the water, stuffed, presumably, with ground-up kava. This is how they make the brew today. One of the elders who spoke a few words of English explained that in the old days, the drink was made by the village virgins, who chewed the kava and spit into a bowl. I was grateful for the change.

Village in Ono

The atmosphere was jovial, with big smiles all around. My smile most likely revealed my insecurity. What were we in for? Soon we were joined by two more village elders and a couple from another yacht. A small bowl appeared, was dipped into the big one, and passed to the most elderly. He swigged the contents, clapped his hands, and said, "Marta!" (Empty.) Presumably this signaled his approval of the brew. Now the same bowl was passed, one at a time, to each person around the circle. When it was my turn, I wondered, Would I grimace? Throw up? Embarrass myself? The communal container would certainly spread any pathogens between the two societies, and the villagers would be more tolerant of any bug in the mix than I. Nevertheless, there was no going back.

Finally the bowl came to me. With a deep breath, I downed it as fast as I could, clapped my hands, and said, "Marta!" Proud and relieved that I had succeeded, I could pause and reflect. It tasted as you might imagine: like the bark of a tree ground up in water. Not great. It would never compete with beer or wine, but was tolerable as part of the larger experience. The bowl went around the circle and came back time and again. I was grateful when the elder called a halt. The effect? It is supposed to be hallucinogenic. That's the goal of those who consume it regularly. I noticed only a mild numbness around the mouth and a dry throat—hardly a reward worthy of the effort. Later, particularly in the big towns, we saw many men who had had too much kava, both short-term and long. It gets to be habit-forming.

The island of Ono had more to offer than a bad taste, and the bad weather only increased the appeal of its harbor and village. The weather was stormy, yet everyone we passed gave us friendly waves and greetings. We were invited—and went—to church. The service was conducted in Fijian, making us miss any theological philosophy. Another day, a lady insisted that we follow her to her hut and sign her guest book. It must have had 200 signatures. It was her pride and joy.

One dark and stormy night, *Chandelle* swung at anchor while being pelted with rain. Pat and I had just finished dinner below when we heard a knock on the side of the boat. What in the world? Dashing up on deck, I peered over the side. I saw a dugout canoe with four teens aboard: two boys and two girls. Could they come aboard? If we had been in the Caribbean, I'd have said no. Here in Fiji? Absolutely.

After tying off with a stout and long line to keep their canoe from hitting *Chandelle*, aboard they came. We had few words in common, and conversation was strained. We gave them soft drinks and cookies. After minutes passed, they began to sing. Hymns. Four-part harmony. They sang in Fijian and they were good. How I wished I'd been able to record them and had my barbershop quartet from home to respond.

Next day, we followed several grownups along a narrow path through dense jungle to a school three miles away. What a pleasant atmosphere. The kids, though shy, were always smiling. There was none of the noise I associate with a school in the U.S. The children were barefoot, but wore attractive uniforms. (In the villages, grownups went barefoot most of the time.) Energy and bodies testified to a good diet.

In many Third World societies, one wonders how a good education can be rewarded, but in Suva and other towns in Fiji there were jobs in shops, construction, and business. The chief in the village of Ono was third in line to be chief. He had two older brothers who had chosen to renounce their right to chiefdom to go to Suva and get into business. The one we met, Meety, was junior and had to stay home to fulfill his family obligation to be chief. He lived in poverty by our standards, but a comfortable poverty with adequate housing and plenty to eat.

It would have been easy to spend weeks at the harbor in Ono. It was pretty, provided protection from weather, and had friendly people. However, the charts indicated another perfect spot at Dravuni, an island farther north. We reached it after a three-hour sail and found four yachts already there. It was sublime: a perfect sandy beach backed by palm trees and no inhabitants. Only the other yachties marred the pristine environment. Then a cyclone warning came in over the radio. A big one was headed right for the Fiji Islands. Everyone began stowing dinghies on deck and pulling anchors for a dash back to Suva. We were about to do the same, when Pat said, "Hey, the harbor there isn't great. Can't we find something as good around here?"

As our friends tore off, we looked at the chart and found a little cove on the main Kadavu Island called Kavala Bay. When we arrived, we saw that another yacht had made the same decision. That was a comfort. The boat was named *Kalahari* (for the desert they said their bank account looked like after the boat was finished) and was sailed by a New Zealand couple. While waiting for the cyclone to decide what it would do, we hiked, dined together, and had a great time.

The cyclone swerved and passed by without hitting Fiji at all. Pat and I sailed back up to Dravuni. No one was there. We spent four days at the island and didn't see another human soul. We swam, snorkeled, read books, and fixed a few things, all at a pace seldom found in this hurried world. For a change, we sailed to a nearby island where some natives were working on their boats ashore. Their boats were fiberglass (disappointing from a tourist standpoint, but giving them a higher standard of living). Constant beaching was wearing holes in the bottoms of the boats, and one had an outboard motor that was jammed from corrosion. *Chandelle*'s locker produced a fiberglass repair kit and WD-40 to big smiles from the natives.

An agreeable daylight sail brought us back to Suva, ice cream, movies, and the part for the water-maker. The yacht club had a bar (surprise), where we met Anne

Bonwit. Friendly and energetic, she claimed to be a sailor (she was) and a cook (that, too), and she agreed to sail with us for four or five days. She stayed three months—all the way to Australia.

The islands continued to provide superb adventure. They looked just like the pictures one sees. The weather was variable, though on average, wonderful. Sailing east to Makogai, Koro, and Savu Savu, we were treated to another school visit, tea in a wealthy native's house, swims and snorkels to rival any, and spectacular anchorages. This perfection was marred by grounding on a reef while we were following waypoints used successfully by another yacht. We were stuck for a few minutes until a puff of wind augmented the diesel enough to get us into good water. It was scary, though. My knees wobbled awhile. There was no one around to help, and coral can easily poke a hole in fiberglass.

Places like Viani Bay, Rainbow Reef, and Taviuni deserve a chapter of their own, but extolling each harbor, island, and swim would be redundant. We had tours with "Jack," an extraordinary local character in Nassau Bay. Words can't do justice to Jack. He was 200 or more pounds of joviality, with a smile as wide as the outdoors. He led us on tours, dives, and to church—all with an infectious enthusiasm for life. (The church service was conducted in Fijian by a man in a traditional robe and bare feet.) We attended a native farewell party and visited a Dutch couple living in the woods. They were raising a few cattle and believed their cows should have a good life before being loaded into the tiny outboard motorboat and taken to market. My imagination creates a hilarious scene of the elderly couple straining to get 500 pounds of beef into this vessel, but they must have made it somehow.

While I was in New Zealand, one of my high school classmates, Holden Clark, called about an impending reunion in Washington, D.C. I could hardly attend; however, he said he did business in the Fiji Islands, buying lumber from a mill for the family plywood business. Generously, he set up a tour of the mill for Pat, Anne, and me and required only that we get there.

The mill was deep in the forest on the far side of the island. Getting there required a long, bumpy bus ride through spectacular mountains—a reward in itself. We were met by the company driver, escorted to the mill, shown our palatial quarters, served lunch with the mill manager and his wife, and given a tour of the mill by the quality manager. After that, we had an excellent dinner prepared and served by the company cook. It was a great day.

Two recollections stand out. First, an American flag was flying on a pole alongside the Fijian flag. When we asked why, we were told it was because of the American visitors: us. Second, OSHA (the U.S. government's Occupational

Safety and Health Administration) would have gone bonkers at the plant's lack of safety features. We watched one log get loose and nearly break a worker's leg. No one worried about it. Workers and legs are cheap in Fiji.

Holden wasn't able to visit the mill when we were there; however, I had promised him a short cruise on *Chandelle* in compensation for the tour. (Later, he may have wished his compensation had been no cruise.) We picked him up in the town of Savu Savu. Although he was wearing street shoes and carrying too much luggage, he was game and contributed what he could, mostly by staying out of the way. We planned several days of downwind sailing through channels and islands, counting on good weather. It wasn't.

It was now mid-July—winter—and weather was brisk. The days were overcast with a little rain and a lot of wind. Thirty knots of wind was common. That's not bad, until you have to navigate narrow passages unerringly, with poor charts and no navigational marks. Sailing overnight was impossible. We had to find an anchorage the first night. Given the wind direction, nothing on the chart looked promising, except for one cove. There was scant information on it, but no alternative. Motoring in to what seemed the best spot, we anchored. And worried. The wind was still strong, and we were less protected than I'd hoped. The cove was too small for extensive scope of anchor chain. The rocks right behind us allowed no time to recover if the anchor dragged. We seemed to be holding, but in good sand? Mud? On the edge of a rock that was about to break off? I stayed in the cockpit for over an hour with my pulse rate high and my hand near the start button.

The anchor held.

Our goal was the island of Yadua. The big harbor shown on the chart was confirmed on the radio by friends who were there. From our cove there were two possible routes to Yadua, both through rocks and reefs. One was shorter, but tricky. The other was longer, but looked easier to navigate. GPS was no help. The charts, such as they were, were not well-correlated to GPS and could be a mile or more off. I chose the longer way. With charts in the cockpit and all hands looking for rocks and any navigational information, we picked our way. Entering the harbor late in the day, we found it to be as perfect as expected: fairly large, high coastline, plenty of room for the four or five boats that were there, and good anchoring depth. We made it our home for four days.

The only major village on the island was on the far, upwind, side. I never found out why. It could have been availability of fresh water; it could have been for a religious or spiritual reason. One day a group of us from several boats walked across the island to the village. The trail took us through dense jungle, over a hill with wonderful views, and eventually down to the beach. Grass huts announced the village. First to see us were a couple of eight- or nine-year-old boys who then ran off. To warn of our imminent threat? Not sure, we continued and found the warmest welcome of the trip. We were soon surrounded by 20 laughing youngsters all wanting their picture taken. Behind them, grownups of all ages were only slightly less ebullient. The kava ceremony, more formal than most, took place inside the chief's house and included many speeches in Fijian imploring the gods to be kind. Once the formalities were over, we all roamed among the huts, finding conversation easy with old and young because most had enough command of English.

This was one of the larger villages and the natives were unusually friendly, even by Fijian standards. Although we could have spent days, even weeks, learning about their society and customs, we had to move on. Holden Clark was running out of time and enthusiasm for this bizarre life. Another yacht, *Mr. Kiwi*, agreed to take him to the main island to meet his plane. That suited everyone.

Now back to our regular crew, we sailed west and downwind to the Yasawa Islands. My notes bring back memories of many great sails, spectacular harbors, walks on isolated beaches, buying shells in this village, visiting a cave in that, swims and snorkels most days, and always the same friendly Fijian welcome.

Once, Anne and I returned from a walk about noon and sat on the beach, wondering where Pat had gone. One of the ladies in the village came up to us and asked—demanded?—that we follow her. What had we done wrong? Without conversation, she led us through the village, which seemed unusually quiet, and finally to a house (grass hut). Inside were nine or 10 people having lunch. We were invited. Sitting on mats on the ground, we were passed a bowl of fish, rice, and vegetable stew delightfully flavored with coconut milk and other spices. We ate with bare hands (there were no spoons). It hit the spot. Anne and I attempted compensation with a Duncan Hines cake we made later, a can of corned beef (part of our emergency supplies and popular in this part of the world), a ball of string, and some fishing line. This seemed inadequate, though all we could do and happily received.

Meanwhile, Pat had had his own adventure. Wandering along a local beach, he was hailed by a village elder. The language barrier limited conversation, but eventually, at lunch time, the elder offered food. Pat watched as his host caught a few crabs and lit a fire with no matches. Pat ate the crab parts familiar to him and the elder ate the rest, including the eyes and insides. This elder had skills likely lost to later generations.

Thus passed our weeks in the Fiji Islands.

During this time, while monitoring the radio on Channel 16, as we always did, I heard a weak "Maidai" (Mayday). Because it was weak, it was likely far away. With no other information, there was nothing we could do. Later, we heard the story. It was the yacht *Camelot* that I had known in Whangarai, sailed competently by Bill and Jan. They were heading to Yadua, and where I had taken the long, cautious route, they had cut the corner and hit a reef. They were unable to get off, and their frantic calls to a tug in a nearby harbor were to no avail because the owner couldn't be reached for permission to help.

Night threatened, weather worsened, and other friends, Don and Mimi, who were standing by on their boat, *Silver Cloud*, took Bill and Jan off. In the heavy weather, that in itself was a dangerous feat. Now in darkness, with no navigational aids, *Silver Cloud* faced the same danger as had *Camelot*.

At anchor in the harbor at Yadua, our friends on *Sunrise* had heard the radio calls. While it was still light, they had put a small strobe light, attached to a life vest, on a dinghy anchor by the harbor entrance so the rescuing boat could avoid a reef and reach the harbor safely. The next day the foundered boat was located in 50 feet of water. Pounded by weather, she had fallen off the reef into deep water and was unsalvageable. We knew all the actors involved in this tragic scene, and *Camelot* was about the best-equipped and best-built boat one could have. This could have happened to any one of us. It was a sobering thought.

It was now late August and loyal friends Bob and Louise Messner were flying halfway around the world to meet us. Pat had volunteered for six months of crew duty, and I had promised to get him to Australia. After mountaineering in New Zealand for three months and sailing in Fiji for three more, his six months were gone. He made no complaints, but had to fly to Australia to catch up to his plans. To make room for the Messners, we took Anne back to the friend she was staying with in Suva when we met her. She would later return to *Chandelle*.

Neither Bob nor Louise was fond of heavy sailing, so *Chandelle* wandered the western Fiji Islands a second time. The repetition was not painful for me because new harbors and coves were numerous and the area has many resorts. Sampling their culinary offerings seemed essential. One village had promised me a great feast, which I thought the Messners would enjoy. The village had quoted a price far higher than an advisor had said was appropriate. I agreed to pay only what I was assured was the going rate. The result was the traditional feast. The cooks make a bonfire to heat rocks, then bury the heated rocks with the food. The result can be spectacular. Although they set an attractive table for us with flowers, etc., the food at this event was disappointing. The fish and crabs were OK; the chicken had been too long on the free range.

The Messners are great friends, and sailing with them was a delight, but their arrival meant missing Fiji Island Race Week, run by the Musket Cove Resort and Marina. Instead, we got a full report. Alcohol flowed, of course, but otherwise the festivities had a unique flavor. There were wet T-shirt contests, costume contests, water fights, dinghy races, and our own Anne won the women's event for tying the fastest bowline. In the final event, the race to Port Villa, Vanuatu, a boat might be handicapped because the crew wore foul-weather gear that matched top and bottom or given extra points for hanging plants.

During our wanderings, we entered a channel that I'd been through before but that now looked strange. There was a large white shape that didn't look familiar. Had I missed the proper channel? The shape turned out to be the hull of the yacht *Rock Steady*, which I had known in the harbor in Whangarai, New Zealand. They had become confused during a rain shower three of four days before, hit the reef, and were unable to get off. The crew was rescued, but here was another case of "Shit happens."

Time marched on. Louise traded a bobbing sailboat for a smooth 747 and the comforts of home in Vermont. Anne came back on board, and after the usual array of fixes, which included hauling *Chandelle* to repair the keel damage done in the grounding months earlier, we put to sea for a four-day leg to Port Villa in the country of Vanuatu. We expected an easy downwind run of about four days. Instead we had strong winds, heavy seas, and no one felt well. I knew Bob was struggling, and perhaps out of sympathy, I was feeling poorly. On the last day, the skies cleared, the winds calmed, and life was good again. We reached port at 5:00 p.m.

16

Vanuatu and on to Australia

Vanuatu is a separate country with its own currency and administration. It is more primitive than Fiji. The only town we saw with such amenities as electricity was the capital, Port Villa. Since the French had recently run the place, we found good bread and two good restaurants. The one street by the waterfront had tourist shops and ice cream; a market, not exactly "super," had essentials. At the inevitable bar by the dock, we met the manager of the local brewery. We got a tour and free samples.

Wilderness beckoned, and after a few of days we set off north to explore more of the islands. Our first stop was Hideaway Island, a nearby cluster of trees and beaches frequented by locals. Next morning, as we prepared to go ashore to snorkel, we saw that the boat next to us had dragged its anchor off the sand shelf and was drifting across the bay toward a lee shore. The owner—I knew him well—and his wife and child had gone ashore to swim. What to do? I could reach his boat with my dink but could I turn on the diesel and operate the anchor windlass? Best to see if I could reach him before his boat went aground. I dashed ashore and frantically looked for him in the crowd. Grateful, he raced to his boat and reached it in time.

On we went to Lamen Bay on Epi Island. There, a 1,200 pound dugong (a relative of the manatee) had grown accustomed to the company of humans. We found him. Snorkeling down, we stroked his back and tickled his flippers. He seemed to love it. For us, it was quite a thrill.

Vanuatu and on to Australia   75

Village Dancers, Vanuatu

In Baie Banon on Malakula Island, the native men put on a dance-show for us and other yachties. (There were six or seven boats in the harbor.) One native knew some English. His explanations made the dances more interesting. One dance was for a birth, another for a wedding, another for a death, another for a new chief. Some were fast, others were slow, but to me they were just a lot of stomping around. Costumes varied from complex coats of grass and masks to less than nothing. Though the village was primitive, all its inhabitants were friendly to us. During the dances, a friend whispered in my ear that the pot to boil a tourist was probably nearby. I had the same feeling.

The women put on a dance for us, too. In grass skirts and nothing else, they stomped around like the men. A feast followed. As in Fiji, heated rocks were buried with the food. The villagers had been persuaded to get into the tourist business. They were building grass huts to accommodate tourists and were getting takers.

A guide on another boat had been living in the area for years. He told us that Malakula Island was comparatively large (roughly 15 miles long) and had about 15 villages. There were few trails and no communication village to village, except wife-stealing and fights among warriors. Over time, languages had become so different that even an outsider could distinguish among them. For example, one language used a lot of *o* sounds; another, a lot of *l*'s—an interesting study for a linguist.

Now it was late September and cyclone season threatened. Although there was more of Vanuatu to see up north, we had heard of the Maskelyne Islands as a do-not-miss. They were an easy day-sail away and as beautiful as anything we had seen. A small archipelago, they afforded idyllic anchorages, which we shared with three boats we knew well.

Eventually, we had to return to Port Villa to check out of the country. Our time-pressures and plans differed from those of others, and we had to leave friends we might not see again. Against this possibility, we had good dinners ashore and long goodbyes at the bar.

At the bar, we heard of a native celebration with dances and the slaughter of a pig. It was a different tribe from the one we had seen on Malakula Island. Though the dances would be similar, the pig slaughter was something different. While I knew it would not be appealing, I wanted to witness it as a "native experience." The poor pig had been selected and confined to a tiny pen by the dance grounds. It knew this was not a good day for pigs. It squealed and cried repeatedly. As the culminating event approached, the pig was brought out of the pen with a short rope tied to one hind leg and another rope tied to the opposite front leg. By tugging on either, its keeper could topple it to the ground. The pig's cries increased. With all the sympathy I had for it, I knew that 50 years ago, in its place would have been a warrior from another village or perhaps a European. In the native language, the word for *European* means "long, white pig." Local records show that a tourist was indeed consumed as recently as 1967.

The pig's final moment was the responsibility of the resident chief. Elderly and frail, he could only batter the beast a few times while it squealed. Eventually a younger warrior dealt the fatal blow.

Our next goal was the island of Tanna, not for native dances or pig slaughter but to see a volcano. Tanna is an island in Vanuatu with no administration. We needed special permission to stop there. After checking out at Port Villa and a tough, overnight slog to weather, we passed the rocky harbor entrance just before sundown the following day. A good night's sleep and we were off to find the volcano. First, we found a native with a vehicle resembling a car to take us up the mountain. He parked several hundred yards from the top and pointed up the hill.

All seemed peaceful save for a strong sulfur-dioxide smell. A few people were standing around the top, but nothing dramatic was evident until we got to the edge. In the instant of peeking over, we were stunned by sound. The huge roar of gasses escaping at high pressure sounded like two freight trains passing close on both sides at high speed. That was one of two calderas. The other, although less noisy, had red-hot lava boiling at the bottom. Once every minute or so a chunk the size of a human head was thrown high in the air to about the level of us tourists. About every half-hour, a chunk the size of a car was similarly ejected. OSHA would have had a fit. There was no guardrail, just loose, black sand. We were told that some months before, a guide had stepped too close, and with no hope of saving himself, had slid all the way down the side into the fiery cauldron. Before that, a tourist had been killed by a rock thrown high in the air that he had not seen. We paid close attention.

Later, as we walked the beach, a native showed us the laundry and stove. The "laundry" was a hot spring, just the right temperature to put your hands into for a second. The "stove" was a hot spring at just below the boiling point, which the locals used routinely for cooking.

In early October, the weather grew warmer and more showery. Cyclone season was approaching. A cyclone was reported 400 miles north of us; we had to get out of this part of the world.

Our next leg began with brisk but favorable winds—until they died. We motored for hours, then the winds went southwest, right on our nose. For the last day and all of the last night, we were hard on the wind, bashing to weather. Anne was handling it well; Bob Messner was not, though both were standing their watches. There was considerable water coming in somewhere. It was not serious so long as the automatic pump could handle it. However, the automatic pump became air-bound (or something), and we had to use the manual pump. That meant pumping the handle under the cabin floor. I couldn't ask Bob for help; he was unhappy enough, whether in the cockpit or in his bunk. I didn't feel right asking Anne. So I pumped about every half hour. No sleep.

Just after dawn, we entered the channel on the south end of New Caledonia. Our three exhausted bodies couldn't have been happier. We changed direction, and the winds were now on *Chandelle*'s stern. The water was sheltered, the sun was bright, the leak had stopped (it only developed under substantial heel), and the country was beautiful. Life was glorious.

We took a slip in the marina in Numea, the main town. Bob had promised to stay with me until Australia, but he had had such a battle with *mal de mer* that I suggested he split from here; I didn't want him to associate me with pain and suffering. He took a few nanoseconds to decide. Before he left, we toured a small part of the island by rental car. The part we saw convinced us that we had seen the best of the island by boat on the way in.

It was now late October. While waiting for a good forecast (weather in the Tasman Sea, which lay between us and Australia, had a reputation for being bad at this time of year), Anne and I checked out the aquarium, the arboretum, and a concert by a local (amateur) chorale and orchestra. As in New Zealand, the chorus was OK, but the French horn wandered off key. We weren't picky. We enjoyed it.

One day, on my return to the boat from a sortie to town, I found *Chandelle* festooned stem-to-stern with balloons. What on earth? Anne had discovered that it was my birthday and had organized a party. Twenty neighbors came by. During the event, a quiet young man who had been sailing on another boat asked if he could go with us to Australia. I was reasonably confident that Anne and I could manage, but a third hand makes watches so much easier. I signed him up. Andrew Fischer turned out to be competent and delightful. We had good conversations. I had hoped to stay in touch with him, but he never responded to the messages I later sent.

Our best source for weather forecasting at this time was a ham operator in New Zealand. The reputation of the Tasman Sea being what it was, we and a dozen other yachts hung daily on the forecaster's every word. For several days, he predicted storms in our area, which as showers and squalls came through, local weather confirmed. Finally, one evening, with a storm sitting right on top of us, he said, "This is as good a window as you will get this time of year." We and a dozen other boats topped-off stores, paid dockage bills, and early the next morning, threw off mooring lines to head for various parts of Australia.

There were three ports of entry. I decided on Mooloolaba as a final goal. Its yacht club had a great reputation, and friends were planning to be there. This made Brisbane the closest POE (point of entry). Although the entrance to the river was tricky—reefs, sandbars, channels—several of the boats leaving with us knew the place well. I figured I'd just follow someone in.

Starting a trip of several days, I felt again the inevitable apprehension. What would the weather do? What gear would break?

The wind was brisk on the beam as we left port, giving us all a good start. Wind lessened before nightfall and shifted aft to put us on a broad reach. It held, thus, for five days: never more than 20 knots, never less than 12. We never motored and never reefed. We hardly touched the autopilot. This was sailing at its best or at least at its easiest. My only problem was that *Chandelle* turned out to be the fastest boat in the fleet. We reached the entrance to the Brisbane River first. It being nine o'clock on a beautiful, sunny morning, we led the procession in with no trouble. As if to welcome us to Australia, two dolphins jumped fully out of the water right by the boat. We were going to enjoy this place.

Check-in went smoothly, until we got to Customs. A charming, smiling man came aboard with a huge, blue plastic bag. He proceeded to load into it practically everything in our freezer and fridge. Australia is proud and protective of its beef industry and takes no chances on pathogens. Tears streamed down our faces when he picked up the particularly good-looking and expensive steaks we had found in New Caledonia. Seeing our distress, he said, "If you will cook and eat them *now*, you can do so. I will come back shortly to check." We did, he did not. All was well.

Brisbane was a motor up the river. We found a group of yachts moored to pilings against the substantial current. We nestled in between the last two. The cost was $2 a day, and we were right in the middle of downtown.

I had expected a tough, industrial town. Not so. Brisbane was pleasantly touristy, with lots of high-end clothing shops, jewelry stores, movies, and ice cream. Our mooring was right next to the city park. Green trees and birdsongs greeted us regularly and several wedding parties chose the area for their ceremony. A good choice for them, a perfect spot for us.

Andrew hopped a plane home to New Zealand. Anne and I sampled the town and the local zoo. Yachties feel superior to the average tourist. Still, we succumbed to sitting with kangaroos trained to tolerate being stroked by children (and adults), and we had our picture taken holding an unenthusiastic koala bear.

I was eager to get to Mooloolaba to be sure I had a dock. I had called from New Caledonia to reserve one, but was not convinced it would be available when we arrived. A weather check (now by phone) and we were off down the river: first to an overnight anchorage, then on up the coast. The weather looked more threatening than was forecast. A mile away we saw two simultaneous tornadoes. I pulled all sail down, moved everything off the deck, and motored away at full speed. As the tornadoes died out, so did my apprehension. We reached Mooloolaba and our assigned dock in good shape.

A new era was about to begin.

17

Roaming Australia

Mooloolaba. It's a funny name but a great place for living on a yacht. A concrete, floating dock in a landlocked body of water makes for a lower heart rate and a great night's sleep. I was in a genuine yacht club that had an appropriate clubhouse, a bar (surprised?), friendly members, and several other yachts on long-term cruises from countries around the world. Wherever yachts collect, so will shops and support services. This area had some of the best. We arrived in early November (spring). In summer, we found relief from the relentless heat by walking 200 yards across a park and road to swim in the ocean off a fine beach. A 10-minute walk up that road led to a fish store, where we could buy fish to either eat there or take home. Ten minutes the other way was a restaurant specializing in huge steaks, salad, and the food and entertainment staple of that continent—beer.

Anne departed to meet a long-time friend, and I settled into my new life. My year and a half in New Zealand had been delightful, but to continue sailing, I had needed crew. Here was the same situation. Selling the boat was always an option, but an unattractive one. I had been lucky in the crews I'd had. There were so many horror stories of incompetence, drunkenness, and thievery that I knew my luck could run out. However, if I stayed here a year and a half, I could do a thorough search.

One morning, lying in my bunk as my brain returned to consciousness, I considered the advantages of finding a young woman—a movie star-type—with a passion for the sea and for cooking. Staggering to the head to wash, the apparition in the mirror propelled me back to reality. I was now 69. Not only was I getting older, I'd been sailing recently with two crew. Having a third person was a big advantage for standing watches. Suddenly, the idea of a couple popped into my head—a couple who were compatible. There are few things worse than being with people who bicker at each other. This in mind, I put an ad in a magazine, the local equivalent of *Cruising World,* and waited to see who would turn up.

Now, with a large continent to explore, a year and a half to do it in, plus errands and local activities, I wanted a car. A couple on another yacht were about to leave and were selling their old Ford. I paid them too much for it, but the thing did well for the time I needed it. At the end, it fell apart from rust. A friend said later that with one more hole, it would have made a good chain-link fence.

Chandelle was in good shape. We had done a lot of hard sailing, yet arrived in port with all essentials intact. I was proud of her. There were, however, 20 items on my to-do list. One project was to replace the steering cable, which by now had withstood 15 years and 30,000 miles. Only a small portion of the cable could be inspected and lubricated properly. Aware that steering cables break, I had a spare. (Why use an old one with a new one in the box?) It's possible to change the cable at sea, but the process is tedious even at a dock. While replacing it, I found that the old cable was still good, but a pulley almost impossible to inspect was not. It could have broken at any time and caused a major failure.

The cruising kitty (monetary type) was OK, since several months had passed with little opportunity to spend. So, in addition to the car, I bought a new radar and a new jib. All three were good investments, and all contributed to the local economy.

While in Mooloolaba, I developed a substantial medical problem. One day, feeling fine, I was having lunch with a local sailor at the yacht club. When we parted, I suddenly had an overwhelming desire for a nap. By dinnertime I knew something was wrong. My only symptom was extreme fatigue. After struggling to get some dinner, I slept many hours, but awoke feeling no better. After several days of constant rest, with just enough energy to open a can of beans or a box of cereal, I struggled to a doctor.

From blood tests he concluded that I had a virus, of which he knew three that would cause such fatigue. It was likely from a mosquito bite, but I did not have malaria and was not contagious. The only treatment he could recommend was to drink lots of water and rest. I could do little else.

Friend Bill Winters was due to visit in a month. I warned Bill of my condition, but he was determined to come. The plan was to drive around the countryside in my car. He was willing to do all the driving, and I could snooze the trip away. Thank goodness I had no sailing obligation. When Bill arrived I felt much the same; however, we set off and toured the southeastern part of the country, including Sydney, one of the handsomest harbors in the world. By the end of the trip I felt better, though walking more than a few hundred yards left me exhausted.

I had scheduled more visitors. Back in New Zealand I had met on a mountain top, Beth Pratt, then 27 and a professional geologist. We'd had several delightful chats and she had taught me good geology. As we parted, I'd said something like, "If you ever want to go sailing…," to which she'd responded, "I do." We'd swapped addresses, and on arrival in Australia, I made contact. She asked if she could bring her boyfriend. I said that was fine with me, but I was genuinely concerned about my health. Could I handle things? Could I get things ready? There were several items the boat needed. I called Beth and expressed my concerns. They were so eager to come, and I had forgotten the energy of youth. They arrived for a three-month visit and fell on the tasks like wildcats on a carcass, wielding drills and hammers, running wires…. The list of projects vanished, while I merely supervised.

Part of the joy of our trip was spending time with two delightful members of that generation. He, Mike Lovejoy, wore earrings. Beth did not. Both loved the outdoors and had the energy to attack it. We all had philosophical differences. A glass of wine at anchor led to great discussions. They were good friends, learning much about each other. Was I a catalyst or a hindrance? I was in touch with them for some months after they left. Eventually, they separated. Perhaps the intensity of life on board brought out problems (not evident to me) that urged them in different directions. Making a long trip on a small boat is a good way to sort out a relationship.

It was now March 10 and the end of the cyclone season. With good, relatively calm weather, we started up the coast for the Whitsunday Islands. Allowing plenty of time for stops, we hoped to reach the Whitsundays in two months. Although my energy was still low, I was making progress. The "kids" did all the work they could: shopping, cooking, rowing, pulling anchor, setting sail; they ran the ship and were good company to boot. With no time-pressure, we stopped at towns and resorts, walked beaches and hillsides. Australia has one of the finest coastlines in the world, with many islands and reefs, including the famous Great Barrier Reef. All enthusiastic snorkelers, we were over the side or off in the dinghy almost every day. The trade winds were behind us, the sailing was easy, and I recall almost no rain.

My energy still low, about all I could do was engineer an adventure or two. For one adventure I demonstrated running aground. (No, not on purpose.) The tide lifted us off nine hours later. We also had one bout of bad weather. As we were sailing near the town of Makay, the winds turned nasty. Both chart and guidebook showed a good breakwater and marina. With a 30-knot wind behind us, we motored in. Instead of a marina, we found pilings with all but one pair of pilings occupied. I demonstrated awesome skill in getting the boat positioned so we could get lines around the pilings. The forecast was for worse weather the following day, so we put double lines around the pilings and went exploring in town. Makay may be the least interesting town on the coast of Australia. Most have something to recommend them, but Makay missed out on everything. Mike noticed a movie playing at the only theater and talked us into going. Memory has blotted out its name. It was awful.

A Navigation Problem

Back at the boat, our neighbor in the piling field was a fishing boat bigger than *Chandelle* and much noisier. The generator had to run all night to keep the catch frozen. The captain apologized, and in compensation, gave us some of his stock: the best prawns and scallops I've ever had. We had the captain and mate over for breakfast. The captain was an energetic 30-year-old who kept referring to his mate as "brain-dead cousin." The other member of the three-man crew liked his booze too much. When the boat was in port, he was regularly in jail. When the weather improved, the authorities let him out to go fishing.

Overall, this was one of the idyllic periods of the trip. We never had to sail overnight. There was little rain. Most days were sunny. There was always a different harbor or an island or a town to explore, and the trade winds were almost always behind us. We three seemed—to me anyway—highly compatible.

On arrival in the Whitsunday Islands, we explored for a few days. The Whitsundays had been our goal for so long that I had to show Beth and Mike what the fuss was about. Eventually, they had to depart. It was a sad moment when I left them on a beach by the local town. It had been a wonderful period for me, and I think, for them. Looking back, I hope I expressed my gratitude warmly enough. I was sorry to learn they later separated, but perhaps it was for the best.

Now I was alone, anchored off the town of Arlie Beach, the shore resort by the Whitsunday Islands. Probably the most popular sailing area in Australia, the Whitsundays have been declared a park. Save for a resort or two, the roughly 20 islands are virtually unoccupied, with ubiquitous anchorages protected from most weather. Hardly wilderness, the attractiveness of the area draws many yachts, which support restaurants and boat mechanics. Mostly I anchored out and dinked ashore for provisions, parts, phone calls, and chats with locals.

Now I had returns from my magazine ad. There were two or three responses from folks clearly unsuited for what I had in mind, though they didn't understand that. I contacted four couples, whose letters looked good, suggesting they come sailing with me for a few days here in the Whitsundays. They all leapt at the chance for a low-cost sailing vacation. It turned out to be a low-cost period for me, too, since all insisted on buying the groceries.

They came for four days to two weeks. They peered at me. They peered at the boat. I peered at them. We sailed, cooked, talked—all congenial—but there was no way I'd take on any of the first three couples. One didn't know how to sail. In the second couple, the wife was great; she was attractive and cheerful and insisted on doing the galley work, but he and I couldn't carry on a conversation. His hobby was following cricket. He proposed training me in the game so we could converse on the subject. *Over a period of months?* No way. The third couple was looking for something to do while their 60-foot gold-plater was being built. They were delightful, but neither I nor they could see them stuffed into the relative confinement of *Chandelle*. I was discouraged. Write another ad? Sell the boat?

There was one more couple on the list. By phone, we set up a time to meet on the dock. As I rowed in, I glanced over my shoulder. I saw a man with hair down over his shoulders, beard to match, and a stocky lady at his side. I was not optimistic. I'd have to take them for at least a few days. At the dock we exchanged handshakes and big smiles. They were cheerful enough. Back at the boat, they stored their gear and enthusiasm blossomed. I guessed it would be OK for a few days.

Robert and Delwyn Scurr and I went sailing. He seemed to know his way around a boat and showed skill as a mechanic. He was a construction worker and in great physical shape; she was a nurse in intensive care: a good combination for life at sea. They were charming and enthusiastic about everything. And they could cook. Not least important, they were devoted to each other. By the end of a week I thought that this could work.

They must have come to the same conclusion. Our cruise became more relaxed and fun. Nothing seemed to upset them. Rain, cold, heat—they recognized all as part of the game. Delwyn's tolerance for boat motion was limited and became a concern, but she was determined to be a sailor. Robert had sailing experience and picked up the details on *Chandelle* instantly. Although Delwyn was new to it, she had studied navigation and often tried her hand at it. When I asked for help with, for example, the whisker pole, she would shout, "Me! Me!" and join me on the foredeck. I grew more and more encouraged. We sailed around the islands for three weeks and nothing happened to make me question my decision, nor, I guessed, for them to question theirs.

They and their families were from Brisbane. That's where the going-away party would be so both sets of parents, brothers, sisters, aunts, uncles, and friends could peer at this wild American with whom Robert and Delwyn would soon run off. The event took place months later. Although I remember the intense inspection, everyone was agreeable, particularly the parents, who were proud of their children for being bent on such serious adventure.

Robert and Delwyn had an unusual view of life. Unlike their brothers and sisters, who focused on family, Robert and Delwyn saved their money from two lucrative careers and went on trips of a year or more. They had traveled in Europe and the Mideast, the U.S. and Canada. Travel was their passion. Just what I was looking for.

They had taken a month of vacation, and at the end of our introductory cruise, had had to go back to work. A flood of communication—thoughts, ideas, questions—streamed back and forth between us, our enthusiasm rising.

Complex itineraries and scheduling are generally anathema to cruising. I had had great luck so far, likely from having allowed several days between visitors for repairs, cleanup, and any surprises. My next visitor was long-time friend Judy Orlando. We did more cruising on land than at sea.

Then came Bob and Louise Messner. I was counting on them to get me up the coast to Cairns. It was another fine cruise for me. They had enjoyed the Fiji Islands, and while they may have found this part of the Australian coast less intriguing, they made no complaints. For me, the area offered a lot: islands, bays, rivers, resorts, and solitude. We had great sails. We motored on occasion, but had little rain and no wind on the bow. Three weeks after the start, we pulled into Cairns and the Dolphin Marina.

After exploring Cairns, an up-to-date touristy city, the Messners hopped a plane home to Vermont. In Cairns, I had a month ahead of me to do boat projects, look for crew to get me back to Mooloolaba, and await favorable weather. The trade winds blow consistently from the southeast, which is great for going north along the coast but grim for going south. Conveniently, around October or November, northerlies appear, at just the right time to get folks back to Brisbane or Sydney or wherever. Although northerlies don't blow every day, they blow often enough to make a huge difference in a trip south.

I waited at the marina, did projects, climbed a mountain, went on a dive boat, and looked for crew. My notices on bulletin boards brought several people by. I wound up with two—count 'em, two—22-year-old chicks. They didn't know each other, so I made them spend a day together. Would they get along? Two ladies bickering at each other was the last thing I wanted. They came back from a day on a dive boat laughing and in a great mood. No problem. We finished stowing provisions, and as we pulled away, I heard a wiseguy on the dock say, "That old coot? He won't last two weeks with those girls!"

I fooled him. We had a great trip. Maite (pronounced *May-tee*) Samuel-Ledoc was French Canadian. She had done a lot of sailing and turned out to be a good cook. She couldn't follow the tell-tails on the jib, but she was fine on the compass, and most important, was always cheerful. Sarah Jacobs had just finished law school in London and was taking a trip before facing the demands of the legal world. Although she hadn't a lot of boating experience, she was bright and caught on fast. Soon the girls hoisted the anchor and set the sails without a hand from me. My responsibility was to apply everyone's suntan lotion. There are some rewards for being captain.

We took full advantage of northerlies as they came through and made good time. The girls would not forgive me if I didn't mention the night I anchored too close to shore at high tide. At dead low tide, 4:00 a.m., we began to bump the bottom. Nobody's perfect. That day we made an early start.

I must have dropped a hint that my birthday was at hand: my 70th. I'll long remember the wonderful dinner these two delightful women served in a spectacular cove to recognize the event.

Maite left after a couple of weeks (we were now back in the Whitsunday Islands). She was meeting another boat. I'm not sure whether it was a paid job or a boyfriend. We would miss her. Sarah, assured that this old codger wouldn't molest her, agreed to go on. Harvey, the autopilot, had died again, and we were faced with hand-steering. Having planned no overnights, we could handle that.

We had great sailing, difficult sailing, and adventure. One evening, a couple on another yacht left their five- and six-year-old daughters with us. Their boat was hard aground. In a few hours, at low tide, it would heel dramatically—too dramatically for the kids. So we fed them and bunked them and were relieved when they finally fell asleep. The parents recovered them the next morning to everyone's delight. What yachties will do for one another.

On down the coast, we met other boats and swapped drinks and dinners. To avoid a hard slog offshore, I chose a narrow channel inside Curtis Island that would give us about one foot under our keel at high tide. I had heard of a yacht stuck there for two weeks, until a higher tide floated them off. At anchor, waiting for dead high tide, I was about to pull the hook and start through when a good-looking vessel about the size of *Chandelle* came by, slowed, and since I was flying the U.S. flag (of course) asked if we had been through before. To my response, he said that he had been through 13 times without hitting. Would I like to follow? Seldom has one boat followed another so closely. We never touched bottom.

We had more great sails, the last before a 30-knot northerly. It was a bright, sunny day, and dolphins were playing nearby as the wind kicked us in behind the Mooloolaba breakwater at 9 knots. The channel was so narrow, I had to run the diesel in reverse to keep from hitting a slower yacht ahead.

I was "home" for the cyclone season, which was upon us, but Sarah wanted more sailing. We found her a fine, large yacht going south, and I sadly watched her go. Last I heard, she was hard at work in London and had a boyfriend who liked sailing.

It had been a great several months, but I welcomed the comfort of a solid dock. Anchors don't drag, and weather of any sort seems almost irrelevant. Now it was time for detailed planning of the big trip through Indonesia. Robert and Delwyn had good ideas, such as dried food (they had done a lot of camping) and a cooker that once filled would keep on cooking and stay hot while we swam or hiked on shore. Later, we brought the cooker to shore picnics several times and were the only ones with hot food. Boat work included varnishing, greasing winches and other gear, and bending on the new jib (it looked OK at the dock, but at sea revealed major faults). We also went to movies. Soon it was time to depart.

It was 1999 and the weather was dramatically different from the previous year's. The year before, we had left in March in docile conditions. Now, winds howled and rain fell for days and weeks. Many boats in the marina were ready to go. Concerned about piracy and crime, five yachts planned to cruise together throughout Indonesia. While we waited for better weather, we all did the less-than-essential items on the to-do list that normally don't get done. They got done. We were ready.

We set off with a forecast of improved, if not perfect, weather and lots of Robert's and Delwyn's family and friends on the dock, wondering if they would ever see these two again. The weather was cool, blustery, overcast. Wind direction was favorable, and we had planned an overnight sail the first night. I hated to do that with brand-new crew, particularly since Delwyn's reaction to the motion was unknown, but the alternative—putting in at the tiny channel by Fishers Island in heavy weather—was risky. I had purchased by mail a big container of Stergeron, an anti-seasick pill not available in the U.S. or Australia at the time. She popped one regularly, summoned her copious quantity of grim determination, and got through.

Before we left, Robert had asked if they could bring a container of split-pea and ham soup for the start of the trip. That seemed like a good idea, but when I saw him put it in the fridge, I gave it no more than a passing thought. There was nothing he could have done to add more to the beginning of the trip. The soup had taken three days to prepare. It was delicious, nourishing, and not the least of its virtues, convenient. There was enough motion that no one was hungry. With a big pot on the gimbaled stove, anyone could get a bowl at any time—or not. It was an enormous help in getting us through the first few days.

Abuse of my new crew continued. By late afternoon on the second day there was again no good harbor at hand, so after discussion all around, we sailed through a second night. Midday, the jib halyard snagged a mast fitting, which meant stopping at the nearest opportunity. That turned out to be Wreck Island—not a comforting name. We skirted around to the lee side and anchored. Robert ran me up in the boson's chair to the top of the mast and I solved the problem. But the motion! It was mild at deck-level; at mast-top, gargantuan. Back on deck I popped a Stergeron myself, yet remained woozy for two or three hours.

After sailing several more hours, there was still no good harbor, so we faced a third night at sea. Robert and Delwyn had been on watch together up to this point, but she learned fast and soon we had three confident watch captains. That made a huge difference on major crossings.

On up the coast, we went over ground I had toured before. Familiarity breeds confidence, and crew learned more every day. Robert displayed his talent for fishing, which would feed us well over many months. The weather improved, permitting stops for walks, snorkeling, and visits ashore. We visited a family essentially homesteading on Percy Island. He'd been hired by the Australian government to shoot all the sheep on the island. Instead, he moved his wife and two young children to Percy. His wife grew vegetables, he shot a sheep periodically, and they lived perfectly well. You meet all kinds of people.

It was idyllic traveling. Winds were always behind us; harbors were interesting—some were calm, some roll-y. Many yachts we knew were going the same way, and we ran into friends repeatedly. We did lots of diving on the western side of the Great Barrier Reef. Diving is best on the eastern, open side, but with no good shelter and doubtful charts, I hesitated to take my boat. The year before I had taken a day trip there on a fast catamaran, and once we made Cairns, Robert and Delwyn took a four-day trip to the eastern side. "Best diving of our lives," they said.

Farther up the coast, we made a spectacular stop at pretty Lizard Island, which has a great harbor, a resort, and a reef-research station. The once-a-week lecture was given the day we were there. It was fascinating, but the scientists admitted they know little about reefs.

A friend on a 55-foot motor cruiser he had built himself took everyone he knew in the harbor on a day cruise to a spot in the reef called the "Cod Hole." There, scuba divers who had swum to the bottom (about 50 feet) were nuzzled by 200-pound cod fish, while snorkelers watched from the surface. There were sharks in the area as well. Were they afraid of the cod? Of the scuba divers? Maybe the Australian government bribed the sharks to stay away.

Captain Cook was the first European to explore this area and the names show it: Cook Town, Whitsunday Islands, Thursday Island, Tuesday Island. The location of his grounding in the then-uncharted Great Barrier Reef is well-known. Without charts, a grounding would be inevitable.

As we got farther north, instead of local boats, we saw only boats going "over the top." By this time, we knew many of them: *Briar Patch, Kotic, Fiddler, Cap d'Ore*. All were good friends and would be our harbor-mates many times. Also farther north were places like Lockhard River and Escape River, which had no habitation and were surrounded by mangroves. It was wonderful to be in relative wilderness.

Leaving Thursday Island, the northernmost spot in Australia, we set a course for Cape Wessel, en route to Darwin, our jumping-off point for Indonesia. "Not so fast," said Mother Nature. The Gulf of Carpentaria looks easy because it's sheltered behind a land mass, but it's relatively shallow and a given wind creates huge seas. Although we were seeing only 20 knots on a broad reach, the seas were big and choppy. Suddenly the weather lower shroud came crashing down on deck. It was 3:00 a.m., raining, with lots of motion. I'd lost a shroud in the Pacific, but in daylight on calmer seas. All hands came on deck and Delwyn watched as her husband climbed the mast to the first spreader, then ran a line to hold things together, much as I had done years earlier. She got sick. Her Stergeron and determination finally failed her.

The nut holding the mast bolt had backed off. I had no replacement, so altered course to Gove, a mining town on the coast. With mainsail down to reduce strain, we were still doing 7 knots. Reasonably confident that the mast would hold, we tried to enjoy the sail. Seas were still rough, yet wildlife was plentiful. Four dugongs (that relative of the manatee) went by, then a pod of dolphins—more than a hundred of an unusual variety. They had round noses and looked like dark torpedoes. Three, four, even five would surf a wave right by the boat. Smaller ones, likely young, did somersaults. It was an extraordinary show and revived our spirits, particularly Delwyn's. She was still recovering from watching Robert climb the mast.

Gove was out of the way, but some of our friends had decided to go there anyway to see the sights. We limped in and found a well-protected harbor with a yacht club that had what we needed: a bar and a restaurant. Our shroud problem was easily solved with the gift of a nut from the yacht *Fiddler*. The skipper had a virtual machine shop on board.

We stayed only long enough to tour the bauxite mine, from which the local aboriginals received a decent payment. The town, like the yacht club, had seen better days.

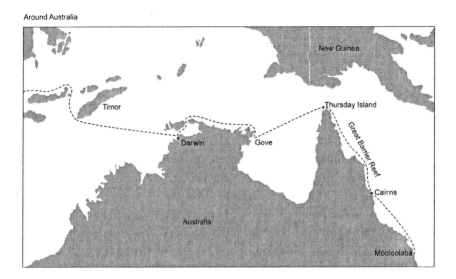

Around Australia

For anyone going west who likes solitude, the north coast of Australia provides many islands and passes. The "Hole in the Wall" pass is a channel only 100 yards wide—probably a crack that formed in an island millions of years ago. We went through with a following current of 5 to 10 knots and had a wild ride. Sailing in that area, we had the wind reliably from the east. When we were ready to drop anchor, the snug lee side of an island or cape always appeared. Australian aboriginals, the only human life, had been given large tracts of land. We saw no one. Having chosen to do this leg alone, we had the area to ourselves.

Next stop was Darwin. As we approached, the tides grew higher, eventually reaching 30 feet. It was like sailing near the west coast of Nova Scotia. Avoiding strong counter-currents, we did one overnight to get past a narrow entrance during a time when currents would be relatively slow, then waited for the lock to open into the marina. With a tide of this magnitude, the lock could only be opened at mid range. The marina fee was substantial. To avoid it, some of our friends anchored out, though they paid for it, if they went ashore for any length of time, by having to haul their dinghy up 300 yards of beach.

Weeks before arriving in Darwin, several yachties had hired a guide to take us on a camping tour of Kakadu National Park, a nearby wildlife preserve. Robert and Delwyn had other interests, so stayed on the boat. For me, it was a delightful change of scene. We slept on solid ground; there were no anchors to drag or docks to bump; the guide did all the cooking and did it well. We were an international community, representing the U.K., Holland, Switzerland, and the U.S. As we hiked, swam, spied wildlife, and bumped along in a cramped truck over rough roads, talk varied from jokes to world events. It was a welcome diversion from cruising.

Back at the marina in Darwin, the new jib arrived, having been re-cut by the loft to a more acceptable shape; the new radar arrived from the repair shop; and the boat was hauled for bottom-painting. All were routine stuff to keep a yacht from falling apart—particularly important before heading to a Third World country.

Indonesia has about 1,500 islands and an understandable desire to know who wanted to visit. The result was a time- and money-consuming visa-application process that took three months of faxing back and forth, wiring money, etc. When all five yachts planning to sail together received their papers and completed their repairs, it was cause for relief and celebration. After a round of drinks at the bar, we sailed off for yet another country.

18

On to Indonesia

Five boats left Darwin together, and they could not have been more different. At 40 feet, *Chandelle* was the smallest, although not the slowest; that spot was held by *Briar Patch,* a 44-foot LaFiet. Making up the rest of the fleet were *s/v Fiddler,* a 55-foot motor-sailor; *m/v Fiddler,* a 55-foot power boat (both *Fiddler*s had been built by Don, now captaining *m/v Fiddler* and a welcome source of mechanical expertise for the fleet); and finally, *s/v Kotik,* a new 50-foot, super-fast sloop built for British owners in New Zealand. Despite our nautical diversity, our personalities worked well together.

At the time, August 1999, there was strife in Indonesia, particularly in East Timor and Ambon, which were sailing destinations. In past years, yachts and crews had simply vanished—likely victims of pirates. The country had serious economic problems and people were desperate. Although we had indications that things were better, our shared concerns brought our five boats together. To avoid Timor and Ambon and the worst of the strife, we headed to Kupang Harbor in West Timor. Here we checked into the country and started the clock on our three-month visa.

Considering the mayhem a few dozen miles to the east, Kupang was upbeat and friendly, though any affluence was kept hidden. We walked, took busses (already overcrowded by half), changed money at banks, visited a museum, and *Briar Patch* found a mechanic to solve an alternator problem. Kupang was not typical of Indonesia.

We headed north, then west along the north side of the island chain to Flores, Sumbawa, and Lombok. The country was gorgeous: steep, lush hillsides covered ancient volcanoes, many of which were active—14 on Flores alone. Small villages consisted mainly of grass huts. Larger towns had a few concrete buildings and an occasional TV dish antenna. On most of our stops, a large dugout canoe came out to greet us. The occupants generally included many children and were friendly, perhaps in anticipation of gifts. We had heard of their desperate plight and had come prepared with soap, paper and pencils, and other such items. Back in Cairns we had purchased a half-dozen used diving masks from a rental shop and passed these out in response to some favor, such as procuring lobsters or a guide.

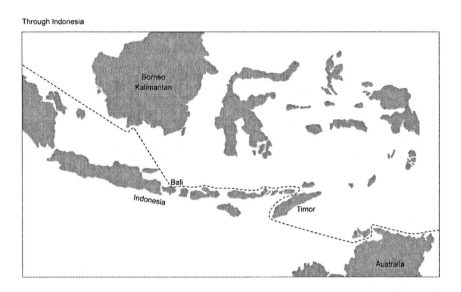

Through Indonesia

It makes me shiver to recall this next event. I nearly lost the boat. Our flotilla anchored off a black sandy beach near a small resort on the island of Flores and went ashore for a few drinks at the bar. While there, the bartender told us of a trip they ran to the top of a nearby volcano. It was a great place to watch the sunrise, so the bus would leave at 4:00 a.m. Yachties can do that. Alarms on all three boats went off the following morning, and leaving our boats at anchor, we bounced along rough roads in the well-used vehicle up to a parking area near the top of the volcano. What a sight. We missed the moment of sunrise; still, the sky was spectacular, and we were surrounded by other volcanic peaks. The volcano we were on had three calderas; although none were active, each had a dramatically different color of water at bottom.

It was a delightful day. We walked around the rims, chatting among ourselves and with other tourists. It was good to forget about boats for awhile. Had I known what was going on with *Chandelle,* I'd have felt differently.

On our return to the beach, all seemed well, with boats swinging properly at anchor. However, on *Chandelle,* something was amiss. The anchor system was tied up differently—not the way I did it—and the batteries were fully charged.

Otherwise, things were as they should be. The next day a large outboard motorboat came by. A man aboard called to me in a German accent. My boat had dragged anchor, well out to sea. A young boy who was nearby in his small canoe had noticed this and had gone to the desk at the resort from which we had toured. They had no boat of any sort and could not help. The boy walked on down the beach to where the German ran a small dive operation. The German put to sea, caught up with *Chandelle,* which was over a mile away by now, and towed her back toward shore. About 80 feet of chain was out, so the anchor caught the bottom well before reaching shore. He had to start the engine—no easy task on a strange boat—raise the anchor, position the boat, and get the anchor back on the bottom. That explained everything.

Flores Island, Indonesia

Profoundly grateful, I offered him a reward. "Don't thank me. We mariners stick together, help each other," he said, adding, "You may want to reward the boy." I gave the boy a healthy amount of cash, and while we were still in the area, each time I saw him, I gave him more cash or the shirt off my back. Had the local villagers retrieved *Chandelle,* they would have stripped her clean in minutes. Even if I had later found the hull, I'd have had no recourse and no option other than to fly home, a dejected ex-sea captain.

A must-see for us was the Indonesian island of Komodo and its famous dragon. However, we were advised of a better tour on the nearby island of Rindja. We sailed into the harbor late one day and at the crack of dawn met our guide ashore. There were dragons everywhere. Three were right by the dock a few feet away. The guide assured us, that like other reptiles, dragons are cold-blooded. Early in the day, they are cool and docile: we could take close-up photos safely. Once warmed up, the dragons can and do catch deer for food. They don't run a deer down, as a lion might, but pounce from behind a bush and wound the deer, which dies in a few hours from the sepsis of the dragon's bite. The dragon follows at a leisurely pace and finds dinner waiting. Without immediate medical help, a human would fare no better than the deer. We followed our guide, walking the island stealthily, quietly, meticulously. I imagined a dragon behind every bush, salivating for a two-legged deer. No humans for dragon food that day.

Of special interest was Bali. Our fleet of five boats planned a two-week stop, and we arranged tours and boat-work on that basis. *Chandelle*'s refrigerator had died and *m/v Fiddler* offered to take our substantial investment in frozen meat until we could have the fridge repaired.

Robert and Delwyn met an old friend and took off to tour. I looked for a mechanic. Although English is not spoken everywhere in Indonesia, with help from a woman at the desk in the marina, a young man showed up who claimed he could fix the problem. He guaranteed it. As I watched him unbolt the compressor to take it to his shop, I wondered first, whether I would ever see it again, and second, if there was any chance he could actually fix it. He spoke no English. I watched him, knowing I had no other choice. *Chandelle*'s crew might eat out of cans for weeks. A few days later, he showed up as scheduled, bolted the compressor in place, charged it with Freon (the kind now illegal in the U.S.), and turned it on. It worked. We chatted through the young lady at the marina desk, who translated, and he assured me his work was guaranteed for 90 days or my money back. Based on his confidence and not wanting to impose longer on *Fiddler*, I retrieved our meat. Then I joined folks from *Briar Patch* and another boat and went off for a five-day tour of the island in our rented van.

Bali, with its rich culture, complex society, and topography of ancient volcanoes, of which Bali High is the most notable, was fascinating. Rice paddies terraced up the steep, lush hillsides. We saw dancers and musicians in one town, Buddhist monasteries and temples in another. Although we had to compete with a plethora of tourists, Bali deserved more than the five days we gave it.

Returning to the boat with three days left before the agreed-upon departure, I found that the fridge had quit and the meat had spoiled. It had to be thrown out and the fridge scrubbed. Why hadn't I left the meat on *Fiddler* until the fridge proved itself? Getting my money back would take too much time. We could purchase ice. We'd be OK.

The two *Fiddler*s chose a different route and our fleet of five dropped to three. Our goal was Kalimantan, Borneo, and the orangutan stations. An overnight sail took us to Baween Island, an isolated spot in the middle of the area. We took a lay day for a good rest, then sailed overnight to the Kumai River on the south coast of Kalimantan. Following the minimal markings, we all made it through the tricky, shallow entrance. We motored five miles upriver to the town of Kumai and began another adventure.

19

Meeting Orangutans in Kalimantan

Kumai had about 20,000 inhabitants. Most construction was wood and single-story. The occasional use of concrete usually indicated a government building. We all anchored on the opposite shore from the town, which seemed quieter and safer, and waited to see what would happen. Although we had made no reservations, the obvious affluence of three handsome yachts meant that our arrival would be noticed. Once our anchors had been down for a discreet length of time, a small speedboat dashed up, and a handsome young native greeted us in excellent English. He would be our guide. Yes, we wanted the tour.

Here was a well-organized business. Our guide set about reassuring us that leaving our boats would be safe. Someone would live aboard at all times and do what cleaning and polishing he could with the materials we provided. The boats would be locked; the guard would sleep in the cockpit and have no access below.

It was worrisome to leave our homes—which collectively approximated the value of the entire town—in the care of these people, but theirs was an established business and the whole town benefited. One incident and all would suffer. We and our boats would be safe.

The following morning, two native boats arrived with crews. These boats were wooden double-deckers, flat-bottomed, and designed to go up the narrow rivers into the heart of the jungle. Each boat had two boatmen. There was one guide for all and one cook. All were young (about 30), and all had big smiles. Only the guide spoke fluent English. With one burner and almost no space to work, the cook prepared Western food for us and native food for the natives. His meals were excellent.

Plumbing consisted of a six-foot-high, three-foot-square box on the stern of each vessel. The box had no top and only enough bottom to prevent a person from falling into the water. No worry about plugged toilets.

Off into the jungle we went. The estuaries became narrower and narrower until we were in true wilderness. We saw many birds and many monkeys, including the rare proboscis monkey. We passed a tiny village, with its houses built out over the water, and finally arrived at a dock and camp.

Sometime in the 1960s, three young women—Dian Fossey, Jane Goodall, and Biruté Galdikas—from the U.S., joined the Leaky Foundation to study primate culture in Africa. Fossey and Goodall stayed on in Africa. Galdikas moved to Borneo to work with the orangutans. There were many young orangutans orphaned by being taken from zoos or taken as pets or because their parents had been killed by loggers. Galdikas developed a successful system for reintroducing these young into the forest so they could live on their own. I was told that she had been on the cover of *National Geographic.* It was her camp we came to visit.

We were greeted by several young natives, a gibbon, and a young macaque monkey. The monkey was a pet and great fun, cavorting from the trees to the ground to my shoulder to someone else's head to wherever. We were here to see the orangutans and were in luck. They were about to be fed. We tagged along to see what that meant. After a half-hour's walk into the jungle, we came to a platform 20 feet above the ground. The natives we walked with climbed up and deposited a huge bunch of bananas and a bucket of milk. Then they banged on pots and pans to announce dinner. They explained that leaving food was not always necessary; however, this year food was scarce. Soon about a dozen orangutans appeared and devoured the offerings. Our hosts further explained that these beasts were from the reintroduced population. The wild ones never approached. They found food on their own.

Some of the orangutans now assembled stayed around to play—happy to climb a leg, ride piggyback, and walk hand-in-hand. They were having a good time, and even though they'd had considerable exposure to humans, for us, it was like communicating with another species. They were friendly, docile, and had a sense of humor. We wished them well.

Unfortunately, their future looked bleak. Illegal logging was devastating the park and everyone knew it. The natives running the reintroduction school were paid and so kept at their jobs. For others, only logging brought food to the table. The central Indonesian government had a park-management department with good intentions, but no money and few staff. Years before, a fund drive in the U.S. had raised $25 million to pay people to start a business other than logging. A check was presented to the Indonesian government with great fanfare, but a year or so later, nothing had been done. Confronted, the government official explained that they had bought an airplane as "the best investment for the people of Indonesia." None of that money went to help the orangutans.

Later, during a tour of the town of Kumai, we saw a building devoted to showing the forest ecosystem and the importance of the orangutans. After we left, we heard that the building had been destroyed by loggers because it was generating too much sympathy for protecting the park. The orangutans are only the most charismatic species there. How many other species will also be destroyed?

This was not a problem we were equipped to deal with. We moved on. After two overnight sails (mostly motoring, often in heavy rain), we crossed the equator and rounded a bend off the coast of Batam Island to see across the water the skyscrapers of Singapore.

Often it's the contrasts that stir the heart. After weeks among the islands of Indonesia, we were inured to poverty. To us the natives looked happy, reasonably well-fed, and adequately housed. To then round a bend in a waterway and see before us the First World—tall buildings, huge ships at anchor, tugboats and ferries dashing about the harbor—sent a shock to the psyche. How can the same animal species live in such contrasting ways? We had seen it before, coming from Vanuatu to Australia, and would see it again, but the sight always had the same startling effect.

Rather than go into Singapore right away, we stayed at the Nongsa Point Marina on Batam Island. Here were the comforts of civilization: a floating dock, shore power, restaurants, and a telephone. Now we had solutions to problems. I called the U.S. for a new fridge.

We were back in the northern hemisphere, but so close to the equator that it was just plain hot: 100°F almost every day. Once the fridge was on order, we could tackle other projects at a leisurely pace. The marina had a handsome swimming pool partially shaded by trees. It was as popular a spot as the bar in any other place, even for yachties. Taking a taxi to town (a bustling yet singularly scruffy place) we got paint, sandpaper, grease, oil, food, and ice cream—all the items necessary for good living. The new fridge arrived (DHL and West Marine make world yachting a pleasure or at least possible) and Robert showed off his mechanical skill. With a small assist from Delwyn and me, he installed the unit in less than two days with marked improvements over the old installation. We were whole again. It was time to leave.

20

Singapore, the Malacca Straight, and Malaysia

It is never easy to leave the security of a well-protected marina, particularly when the weather is blisteringly hot and the marina has a swimming pool. Still, the towers of Singapore beckoned and we were talking on the radio to friends who were there enjoying it.

With only a vague idea of what lay ahead, we tossed the dock lines early in the day. There was little wind, much haze, and lots of traffic—most of it big. Singapore is an island snuggled close to Malaysia. Johar Bahru, a city of 2 million people, crowds one end of the causeway that connects the island to the mainland. We'd heard that it was a good place to anchor. To get there we had to cross the main harbor festooned with huge ships, many of which were underway. The haze made it difficult to tell if a ship was moving or not, but several were moving and coming at us from all directions. One or two seemed bent on running us down. There was no obvious traffic control. Horns honked and the radio chattered, but we couldn't decipher enough of it for any use. After three hours of dodge-'em, we crossed the harbor and motored around Singapore Island to anchor near Johar Bahru. It was a perfect spot: well-protected from weather and right next to a dock for police boats. We could leave our dinghy at the dock and it and *Chandelle* were as safe as they could be.

Our goal was Singapore. After Customs and a bus ride across a long causeway, we were in a First World city, or so it seemed. Heavy fines for jaywalking, jail for littering, and lashings for graffiti were incentive enough to be ideal tourists without also knowing that Singapore executes more people in a year than does the U.S. Whether Singapore qualifies as First World and *free,* I'll leave to others. We saw a clean, functioning, affluent, and interesting city. Many buildings were as new as any in New York. People were well-dressed and apparently doing well. We happened onto the Festival of Lights in the China quarter—a parade with the enthusiasm and noise typical of Chinese culture. At the other extreme was the museum of a WWII Japanese prison, where half the inmates had died of starvation and mistreatment.

After 10 days, we heard the call of the sea. Sailing out into the main harbor, we again dodged freighters to reach shelter in a group of islands that looked appealing on the chart until I noticed the warning: "Do not anchor anywhere in these islands!" They were on our path, so we sailed among them anyway and saw many such signs. With Singapore's reputation for applying discipline, we did not wish to be caught littering with our boat.

It had been a long, tough day, and we were tired. A place on the mainland that looked possible turned out to be too exposed, so we rounded the corner into the Malacca Straight and got hit by a 30-knot headwind. We bashed on under power doing about 3 knots, and at 10:00 p.m., reached the small island of Pu Pisang. We anchored and fell asleep only to be awakened at 4:00 a.m. by a heavy thunderstorm. The anchor had dragged, so we had to reset it; then the wind shifted and we were again exposed. At 7:00 a.m., we left and motored against an even stronger headwind. Unable to make progress, we returned to Pu Pisang. This time, looking for better shelter, we anchored close to shore. We were tired and worried that the anchor would drag again and the wind would blow us onto shore. Instead, the weather calmed. We could rest at last and took a lay day. Yachting is alotta work.

Things improved. Winds became light, and we motored all the next day and night with comparative ease, except that we suddenly bumped something: a huge log longer than *Chandelle* and about four feet in diameter. Luckily, we could see no damage. We called the boats behind us to report the log's position.

We'd heard that a new marina, the Admiral, had just opened on the coast. The security of floating docks well-protected by a breakwater appealed to us, so we put in. The marina manager was a nutcase who bragged about his nine children, all by different women, none of whom he'd married. However, that had nothing to do with the marina he managed. He took such good care of us that we made travel plans.

For four weeks we left the boat at the marina, and all three of us went up into the central part of Malaysia to Taman Negora Park. In the middle of the park and accessible only by bus and a small boat up a long river, was a camp. The camp had tents, a restaurant, and a few guides. Otherwise we were in wilderness. A small group of nomads were camped nearby. Our guide suggested we stay with them for a night. They would build us a shelter, and we could sleep by their fire.

It seemed like a touristy thing to do, but I found a young couple at our camp for company and off we went to see the nomads.

Nomads, Malaysia

It was late in the day when the three of us walked down the jungle path to their camp. We had eaten an early dinner in our own comparatively comfortable camp. A fee had been agreed upon, and we were advised to pay only that. With no idea of what to expect, we entered the little clearing and saw the nomads. I counted 10 adults, all young—20s to mid-30s—and seven or eight children from toddlers to age eight or nine. Five lean-tos surrounded a smoking fire. Two of the men greeted us with warm smiles. The women seemed shy. No baby cried.

One young man, perhaps 25, took charge. He showed us the housing they had built for us, a lean-to just like theirs. We saw a patch of bare ground covered with grass mats under a structure of poles. The structure was covered by more grass laid at a slant to make some percent of rain run off. Our quest for adventure did not include wanting to test the effectiveness of this structure. There had been a downpour the night before.

Although we were unable to make conversation with them, we were invited to sit by the fire as they chatted among themselves. Shortly, an older man walked into camp carrying a long blowgun. They hunted with blowgun and poison darts. All looked quickly at him, to which he shook his head sadly. There would be no monkey (or whatever) for breakfast. We were allowed to inspect his gun. It was a fine piece of carving, mostly bamboo and beautifully decorated. We showed our admiration, and they indicated that they could make a gun and darts for us. They had none to spare, so had to make one specially and under time-pressure. Therefore, the result would not be so finely decorated. Nevertheless, the result remains one of my prized possessions. We spent another hour or so at the fire, during which one man taught us a few words in their language and made a grass ring for the lady in our party.

It was a warm night with no rain, and we slept about as well as one would expect on grass mats over hard ground when used to a reasonably comfortable mattress. Not great. Still, it was a quiet night. No large animals barged into camp. The only sounds came from bugs I could not identify.

Next morning, after handshakes all around and a few pictures, our threesome walked the half-mile back to "civilization." I was scheduled to return to New York that day, so I boarded the outboard-driven watercraft for the trip downriver, took a bus to the airport in Kuala Lumpur, boarded a 747, and after 18 hours, landed in New York. The next bed I occupied was my own. One night in the Stone Age, the next in Manhattan.

I came home for a physical exam, to check on my apartment, and to see friends and family for as long as time allowed. All was quiet on the home front, so back I went to my other world.

The Malacca Straight is one of the most fought-over areas on the globe. The battles among and between the Chinese, Indians, Arabs, English, Spanish, and Portuguese over everything from spices to trade routes fill stacks of history books. The city of Malacca, colorful in itself, houses a museum full of artifacts from many eras. Tragically under-funded and likely missing many of its best items, the museum has paintings, spears, cannon, and other objects testifying to the concentrated mayhem. We sailed in waters that over the centuries have absorbed many buckets of blood.

And thunderstorms. In October and November, black clouds form daily over Java across the way, and by the time they reach Malaysia, the thunder and lightning are as intense as any I've ever seen. The natives shrug this off, but we were living close to a tall aluminum pole. I know of three boats that were seriously damaged; two were close to *Chandelle* when they were hit. We were lucky.

Kuala Lumpur was easy to visit from the marina. Typically for this part of the world, there were huge contrasts in affluence, architecture, religion, and culture. The city is famous for its twin towers, which I understood to be almost wholly unoccupied, but other buildings in the area also expressed modernity and style. A walk in any direction brought us to temples and mosques and all sorts of tiny shops. For food, we always went native. Down a back street, sometimes not even inside, we'd find trays of steaming offerings, some of which we could actually identify. We ate nothing that wasn't hot and never got sick. Friends who tried a fancy restaurant were not so lucky.

The world beckoned, so on up the coast we went to Penang, Langkowi, and finally Rebock Marina in Thailand. We had spirited sailing; some motoring; a few overnight sails; a few squalls; and trips ashore to temples, museums, and repair shops—all the usual components of cruising. We were having a great time. This was what we came for.

At a small field on Phuket Island, we stumbled on an air show. Countries like Russia, the U.S., and France were hawking their wares to local governments. Military jets buzzed the field and performed stunts. Best were the six prop planes from Australia all piloted by women. They did wonderful coordinated flying.

Thailand is one of the finest cruising areas in the world, with warm, reasonably docile weather and picturesque anchoring spots. At the time of our visit, labor rates for boat work and the cost of dinners ashore made Thailand a great value. Many cruisers teeter on the brink of financial disaster, so spending time in Thailand provides a chance for the cruising kitty to grow. Still, the primary attraction is the beauty of the place. Wandering by boat around the island of Phuket, we found islands with caves, small coves with room for only one boat, tiny villages, and small vessels with colorful lateen sails mixed in among the "longtails"—large, canoe-like boats with engines and long propeller shafts critically balanced to permit steering them right onto the beach. The longtails made an awful racket; mufflers weren't considered necessary.

Several of our friends talked of staying in the area for a year. Many cruisers do. People leave their boats to go home; climb the Himalayas; tour Cambodia, Vietnam, Hong Kong, and wherever. My stays in New Zealand and Australia had been so successful, I was sorely tempted. I was stopped by Robert and Delwyn—the realization that they would leave me. Every day they were better crew: more knowledgeable and more adventurous. My chance of replacing them was slim.

This would be our look at the coast of Thailand. Christmas, New Year, and the new millennium were approaching. Although liking solitude more than many people, for major events, yachties long for good company. Christmas found us at Bitam Island along with friends on *Angelique*, *Wilde Goose*, and a dozen fishing boats. Christmas Day the wind howled above 40 knots. Even the fishing boats stayed put.

Chandelle had been the drag queen of many harbors. If anyone dragged anchor, we did. However, at the urging of others, who believed that if my anchor dragged, they were in danger (how selfish), I had purchased a new anchor called a Bugle. This would be its test. It held. Another yacht entered the harbor and tried several times to set their anchor. Unsuccessful, they had to leave in the middle of the storm. *Angelique* raised the "Come Aboard" flag (by radio), and with contributions from others, put on a feast. Good food, good wine, and good company in a boat confidently at anchor with a roaring gale outside. What could be more convivial?

The weather calmed and Y2K Eve found us, along with many friends, anchored off the town of Patong on the west coast of Phuket. We chose this spot anticipating the fireworks for which the Thais are famous. We preferred dinner ashore in a good Thai restaurant to the realities of the town. Among them were tourists who'd had too much alcohol (well, it was Y2K Eve). Worse were the men in their 50s and 60s with 16- and 17-year-old Thai girls on their arm. It was depressing. Best was the view from the boat as we awaited midnight and the fireworks, which were wonderful.

21

Exploring the Andaman Islands

Seldom was my sanity questioned so thoroughly by friends at home than when I explained that now, the crew on *Chandelle* wanted to do something unusual. Understand that we were in a community of people all doing the same thing: visiting foreign countries, crossing oceans, coping with storms at sea. There were yachts like ours almost everywhere we went. Our route to this point was a milk run. What could we do that was off the beaten path? The Andaman Islands were the answer.

We had heard that they were visitable, though not easily. The islands are off the west coast of Thailand, north of the usual cruising route, owned and run by India. At the Indian consulate in Kuala Lumpur, our expression of interest raised eyebrows. The man heading the consulate came out to talk to us. Why did we want to go? Did we realize that it was expensive and time-consuming? We persisted. Later, we discovered the reason for his questions. Three tribes of aboriginals have lived there for thousands of years—according to recent DNA testing, 40,000-50,000 years. To protect these tribes the Indian government has set up procedures that also protect the islands in general. We were sympathetic and intrigued. We filled out extra forms, paid extra fees, and agreed to return to the consulate in three weeks when the visas would be ready.

With visas in hand, after a too-brief tour of the Thai coast, we set sail. Expecting a three-day trip with variable weather, we got lucky and had a fresh beam breeze all the way, arriving in the main town, Port Blair, in two days. Then the fun began. The Indians monitor all ships in the area by central Harbor Radio. They were professional and helpful. After directing us to the anchorage, they called, sequentially, Customs, Immigration, the Harbormaster, and the Navy. Things started badly. We had been warned that Customs officials were hungry, and I hoped the cheap liquor I had purchased would satisfy them. However, straight-shooters Robert and Delwyn persuaded me not to pay a bribe at all. Later, I regretted having agreed.

Two men from the Customs office appeared on shore. I picked them up in our dinghy. Once aboard *Chandelle*, they went casually through our paperwork and the boat. Everything seemed fine until they asked, "What do you have for us?" I explained that we had nothing for them and that all seemed OK to us. They looked astonished. Now they went back over our paperwork and the boat, and this time, they found transgressions: an old camera I had overlooked, a knife, some change. We were supposed to list *all* the items on the boat. Therefore we were in error. I had to see their boss.

This required a short taxi ride through town. It was a fascinating ride. We were now effectively in India, seeing Indian people wearing Indian clothes. It was a new country, and I was nervous. What was I in for? Would I go to jail? The taxi stopped at a scruffy office building where I found the Customs chief. One of the inspectors was explaining to him how we had sinned. For the next half-hour I sat in a chair across from the chief and listened to his tirade on how difficult his job was and how smuggling could ruin the islands. I looked as chagrined as I could and said nothing. Finally, he stamped the papers and let me go. Riding back in the taxi, I relaxed. I looked at the people, their costumes, and their houses without wondering what view I'd have from jail.

It took five days to complete the check-in. Although all arrangements were made by Harbor Radio, the steps had to be done one at a time. Next was Immigration. That was easy. We had our visas and there were no dead bodies on board. Then I had to see the Harbormaster. The Harbormaster had a nicer building than Customs. Nicer yet were the people. First I met the assistant. He was a tall, handsome gentleman with a colorful turban who sat behind a big desk. After a broad smile and a handshake, he ordered tea. An underling brought us two cups. We talked about the weather and my trip over from Thailand. Then it was time to see the Harbormaster himself. He was a taller gentleman, more handsome, with a finer turban who occupied a larger office and sat behind a bigger desk. I wished I'd brought my camera. No tea, but we had a pleasant conversation. He asked how everything was. I said everything was fine. I lacked the nerve to tell him about my experience with Customs.

Finally, we had to be inspected by the Indian Navy. We could go ashore and explore locally and did, but without full papers we could not move the boat. Port Blair by itself makes a great visit. The Indians use the huge, brick Circular Jail to showcase how the British mistreated them in the 1800s and early 1900s. The Indians took umbrage at the British notion that they, the natives, should do all the work for no pay while the British sipped tea and cocktails and enjoyed a life of leisure. Natives who objected were dealt with harshly.

In spite of repeated calls to Harbor Radio, the Navy didn't appear. Another yacht had come in and also wanted inspection. That captain and I got in a dink and motored the half-mile around the harbor to see the Navy and see if we could speed things up. We tied the dink between two large ships and climbed onto the dock. Wandering around looking for someone official, we saw lots of activity. Men in Navy uniforms were running around carrying small arms (rifles and pistols) and boxes marked *ammunition*. No one took any notice of us. Finally, spotting someone who looked like an officer, we stopped him and began explaining our plight. He yelled at us excitedly, "What are you doing here? If you don't get off the dock right away, I'll have you thrown in jail!" Although we had wandered all over the place—walking down alleys, looking into buildings—we agreed to leave promptly. Could he have someone come see us? Grudgingly, he said he would. They must have been planning an exercise (an attack on a Burmese outpost?), and now, because of us, their secret was compromised.

The next day two handsome, amiable, spit-and-polished young officers came to our vessels. They took three hours to inspect *Chandelle*. They looked casually in lockers and on shelves; one of them looked at every page in our radar manual. What he expected to find, I'll never know. Finally, they left. We were fully checked-in and free to roam the islands, although with several caveats. We had to call Harbor Radio twice a day and anytime we raised or dropped anchor. There were places we could go and places we could not. Places were forbidden to protect the aboriginals. We were completely supportive of that.

For anyone who might use these writings as a cruising guide, I've included the names of places we visited so our wanderings can be followed on a map or chart.

Our first stop by boat was to Havelock Island. The only chart we had was the U.S. 63380, which was not adequate. We were able to borrow and copy charts with more detail, such as the B.A. (British Admiralty) charts, and I highly recommend them.

We anchored in good sand in front of a dive shop and campground about a mile south of Doone Point. The dive shop operators were helpful, and we rented equipment from them. We made another stop at the north side of the island just west of a large pier. After buying fruit and renting motorbikes—a good way to see the countryside—we watched elephants helping to pile logs for export onto barges.

Chandelle at Havelock Island, Andamans

From here we went to Minerva Ledge, approximately 10 miles northeast of Havelock. Although we could locate the ledge easily on the chart, finding good sand for anchoring was tougher. We found coral at 35 feet. Looking farther, we found reasonably good sand at 50 feet. There is no protection. The reef is a good five miles from any shore, so weather is an important factor. The weather and anchor held while the diving contingent explored and the boat-watcher watched. Divers reported a good dive.

Late in the day, we motored over to the bay between John and Henry Lawrence islands and found a fine spot on the west side of the southern point on Henry. Good sand, good depth, and calm. Next day we were back to Minerva Ledge. Again we found reasonable sand at 50 feet. This time the divers had one of the dives of their lives. Minerva Ledge is large. You have to explore it to find the best spots, but the effort is worth it.

Our next trip was up the river, or pass, between South Andaman and Baratang islands. Although the river is shallow at the entrance, we saw nothing under 10 feet. Once in the river, 50 to 100 feet was the norm. We saw no people, only an occasional fishing boat. An hour or so up the river is a ferry crossing with a town, Nilambu, on the Baratang side. We found a good anchoring spot 300 yards south of the dock. This town is not touristy and must be short on entertainment. We were watched by close to 30 natives sitting on shore as the best show available. We had lunch and dinner in each of the two restaurants and ate with our hands. Although I don't know what it was, the food was good, and we didn't get sick.

Next, we went a mile back downriver to where the river divides, then up the western leg. Now we were in wilderness, in an area reserved for the local aboriginal tribes. These tribes are a fascinating study. Related to no other culture in Asia, they migrated from Africa thousands of years ago. How did they get to these islands? In any case, isolation is their only chance for survival. Both the Indian government and we endorse this. We made no contact. We anchored in a small bay and explored the large mangrove forest by dinghy: many birds, some fish, no evidence of humans anywhere.

We continued north and found a way west out to the Bay of Bengal. We went late morning at high tide, with the sun behind us and a crewman up the mast. It was not an easy path to find. We spent much time motoring at two knots in the shallow water. Although we saw depths of eight or 10 feet many times, we got through without touching and headed south along the coast of South Andaman. Stay well off. There are uncharted reefs far out. Two miles off kept us out of trouble. For a night's rest we stopped in Port Campbell. There was no port and no sign of human life. We looked for sand on the north side of the bay, behind the small island, and found nothing but coral. We went to the south side and found a good spot. We were still in wilderness.

On the following day we went south to Twin Islands, passing to the east of them and anchoring south of the eastern one. The bottom was coral and sand. Drift-snorkeling by dinghy between the two islands, we saw a turtle, a five-foot manta ray, an octopus, and a seven-foot cod—bigger than anything we had seen in the Cod Hole in Australia. Around the coral heads, fish were as varied and colorful as any we had seen.

From the Twin Islands, we returned to Port Blair. We stopped briefly at Ross Island to see the ruins of the island penal system, run by the British aristocracy for nearly a hundred years. A worthwhile stop. Being British in those days was a good idea.

To check out, the reverse of the check-in is necessary. We employed the services of Joy James, a local agent. Easygoing and knowledgeable, he had just bought a new van, which we used for shopping. He helped us avoid the clutches of the head Customs man, who was planning more harassment. Many yachts use Joy. He can be contacted by Harbor Control.

Yes, it was worth it. Some of the best snorkeling, tamest fish, most interesting natives, and deepest wilderness we had or would experience. But the clock was ticking on life and weather patterns, and we had to move on. We talked a lot in the cockpit and over dinner of the fascination of India. We looked forward to its exotic sights. Little did we know; we weren't going to get there.

22

Sri Lanka—by Mistake

Passing small islands of dense greenery, we left the Andamans through a lovely channel cut between easily seen reefs. The last land mass was the island home of an aboriginal tribe noted for animosity toward outsiders. The aboriginals had been ruled first by the British, who likely treated them badly, then by the Japanese, who likely treated them worse. Years ago the Indian government, trying to protect them, sent an emissary to offer assistance. The natives speared and killed him. The message? Stay away. We sailed past, looking on with fascination, but held course for India.

It was now the middle of January. The Bay of Bengal has fierce weather, though not at this time of year. We started with fine days and good winds and made good time. We even hoisted the spinnaker (repaired in Tahiti). Seas were relatively calm and there was no ship traffic. We had fresh fruits and veggies; occasionally, Robert caught a fish; we were on our way to the exotic land of India. Picture perfect, except for the one veg we'd bought not knowing what it was. Thumb-sized and green, it looked good but made us sick when we put it in a stew. Otherwise, conditions were delightful—as good as offshore sailing can be.

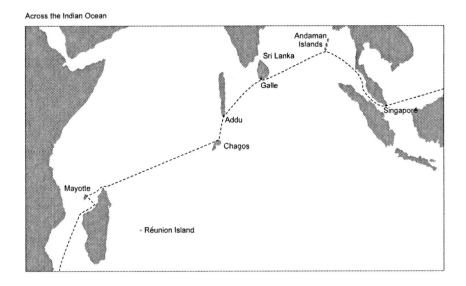

Across the Indian Ocean

Then, right smack in the middle of the Bay of Bengal, the wind died. No problem. We had plenty of fuel. We motored until midday, about 12 hours, when we heard a grinding sound from the engine. The engine kept running, but the boat slowed. Soon, with the engine still running, the boat stopped. We were 400 miles from any shore. Tests pointed to the transmission. It would not drive the boat forward; it *would* drive the boat backward. We discussed the situation calmly and concluded that we were fine. We had plenty of food and water; the engine would still support the batteries and water-maker; from time to time there was bound to be wind. The ancient explorers could do it. So could we. We had advantages Magellan did not: GPS for one. While slatting around waiting for wind, I glanced at the GPS and saw that we were going north at 2 knots, right toward Bangladesh. That was not on our itinerary. We turned the boat around and motored backward at 2 knots. That was as fast as we could go without straining the rudder. Two knots did little more than nullify the current, but at least we weren't going the wrong way.

Instead of India, our target became Galle, Sri Lanka. With wind, we sailed along on course. When the wind died, we dropped sails and motored in reverse. Harvey, the autopilot, handled it either way. To motor, Harvey turned the boat around until we were on course backward. It was amusing. Slow, but amusing.

We had been urged to stay 40 miles offshore around Sri Lanka because fishermen sometimes harassed yachts. We had no choice but to sail for Galle and hope for the best. Approaching the coast backward, we feared being a magnet for attention. A few miles away, we could see a fishing boat off the starboard bow (actually, our stern). The instant they saw us, they pulled in their net, motored toward us, and came alongside. Confined to a speed of 2 knots, we were helpless. Delwyn went below. Robert and I gathered a few items that wouldn't look menacing but could be used as weapons: spear gun, short pipe, a hammer. Robert used his disarming smile. I did my best.

The five men on the boat were not handsome, not well-dressed, not smiling; all were sitting on their rail—now parallel to us and close enough for an easy jump to *Chandelle*. Their captain spoke a few words of English: "Why are you backward? Where are you going?"

He was only a few feet away. I urged him to move farther away: "We captains know how dangerous a collision at sea is," etc.

They finally left, perhaps concluding that we weren't worth the trouble. Though it lasted 15 or 20 minutes, the encounter seemed an hour or longer. It took longer still for our nerves to stop jangling.

As we neared shore, a breeze picked up and took us, going forward, as far as the Galle harbor entrance. There the wind died. The three or four yachts at anchor may still be talking about the crazy Americans who motor into harbors backward.

A new country and new experiences lay before us, but our thoughts focused on the transmission. Robert was about to demonstrate mechanical skill to match his skill at fishing. Wrenches and screwdrivers flew, and the transmission came apart. Delwyn and I checked into the country and went shopping.

Once we had the transmission out of the boat and on shore, word spread that we needed a mechanic. It's amazing how many mechanics appear in a poor country where work is slow. Although eager and enthusiastic, they did not persuade me of their skill. Robert had mentioned doing mechanical work with his dad growing up. His dad was in charge of maintenance for a fleet of trucks owned by a chain of hardware stores. After school, Robert and his two brothers often helped their dad fix a set of brakes, a starter, and yes, a transmission. We had been sailing together for nearly a year. I knew that whatever Robert lacked in experience, he would make up for in diligence. I'll take diligence over enthusiasm anytime (well, not anytime, but definitely in Sri Lanka). My engineering training allowed me to discuss theory and to hand him the appropriate end of a wrench. The transmission went back on board.

To determine what parts we needed, order them from a company in the U.S. (from a phone in a private house), battle Customs at the airport, and reassemble the transmission—testing it at every step—took nearly a month. For most of that time we were stuck in and around Galle. We were delighted to be there, but Galle lacked the desirable features of a vacation spot. In addition, the harbor opened to prevailing weather, resulting in roll-y conditions even with anchors out bow and stern.

Fortunately, there was a Sri Lankan Navy base where we could leave the dink in comparative safety during trips ashore. Because the Tamil Tigers had attacked its ships at night by planting bombs on their hulls, the Sri Lankan Navy used a small boat to drop sticks of dynamite into the water roughly every 45 minutes all night long: a racket loud enough to blow out a swimmer's eardrums. This routine took getting used to, particularly when the dynamite detail, in a spirit of fun, dropped a stick behind a yachtie motoring home after dinner ashore. No bodies floated to the surface; the noise was just part of the color of life in Galle Harbor.

In our ongoing battle with Customs, we were required to go into Colombo, the capital. On the day I was there, after a long period of little or no wind, the profusion of two-cycle motor bikes made Colombo the most air-polluted city I had ever experienced.

The only word for Galle is *shabby*. No one looked wealthy; almost every building needed paint. Traffic on the dusty streets was mostly pedestrian. There were a few bicycles, an occasional truck, and many tuk-tuks—tiny three-wheeled taxis with one-cylinder engines that made a popping sound: "tuk-tuk."

The walk to the center of town from the dock was doable; if carrying any load, the tuk-tuk was a welcome option. The temperature hovered at or above 95°F. Once, when I hailed a tuk-tuk to go back to the boat, the driver went far out in the country despite my telling him he was going the wrong way. When we finally arrived at the dock, he demanded a fee several times the normal amount. I wouldn't pay. He began to shout. A crowd gathered, obviously sympathetic to him. It was daylight; I would have been much less determined at night. People called for policemen, but none arrived. We had a stalemate for 20 minutes until an older man came along. Although showing no wealth or station, he was dignified and could speak some English. (Language had been a useful barrier for the driver.) The older man arbitrated an amount more than I had always paid, but far less than the driver wanted. My impression as I left was of the arbitrator scolding the driver. I think I struck a small blow for the next tourist.

Not all tuk-tuk drivers were like this one. One of the delights of Galle was meeting one in particular. Drivers hung around the dock looking for fares and we hired several of them. With one, we hit it off. Ekka was perhaps 25, always clean, well-dressed by local standards, and handsome. Most impressive of all was that he knew and took us to the best shops, the best hardware store, the best machine shop and welder. We used him a lot—all we could. Robert and Delwyn, as gregarious as anyone and close to Ekka's age, developed a friendship with him.

Ekka invited us to his house for dinner. There we met his wife, who was as beautiful as a model, and their two-year-old daughter. Their home was tiny, one story high, crowded between two other houses, and their pride and joy. Before we left, we took them to dinner at the best hotel. It was on top of a hill, only a half-mile from their house, yet they had never been there. We later heard that to prepare for the event, she had collected suitable clothing from sisters and cousins all around town. She was drop-dead gorgeous.

The tsunami of December 2004 flooded places we had visited. The island of Phi Phi Don was destroyed; Phuket was heavily damaged, as was the coast of Sri Lanka. News reports showed the frightening devastation of these once-beautiful places. What had happened to Ekka and his wife and child?

Robert and Delwyn were by this time living in Australia. They had kept up a correspondence, and about three weeks after the tsunami, they heard from Ekka. Although all three of the family were fine, their house and tuk-tuk were gone. He could rebuild his house, but he would have to buy another tuk-tuk. Could we help? We wrote to friends in the U.S. and Australia and wired money to help put him back in business. As I write, he had received the money and had purchased a used vehicle. We wish him well.

Toward the end of our month in Sri Lanka, with the transmission project under control, we took a five-day trip to the highlands. A short and crowded bus ride took us to the train station and a more-crowded train. Finding no seat, I sat in a doorway with my legs dangling outside. This was no big deal because the train traveled only 12 miles an hour. Our destination was the city of Kandy. High in the mountains, it was more appealing than Galle and cooler. Kandy had modern, as well as fine, old buildings that made us feel safe and comfortable, and the food was better. In Galle, we went to Chinese restaurants because the Sri Lankan food was too spicy. In Kandy, tourist traffic kept the spice gods at bay.

Higher up in the mountains, we came to tea country. We toured plantations, chatted with tea-tasters, and hiked in the cool, picturesque countryside. Now we saw why tourism is big business in Sri Lanka. Our enjoyment overcame our good judgment, and we stayed an extra day. Back in Galle, although conducting our departure activities at a frantic pace—provisioning, fueling, checking out—we nearly got in trouble for overstaying our visa.

One incident in Sri Lanka is worth telling. Craig and Mary on the s/v *Erasmus*, a sloop much like *Chandelle*, were anchored near us in the harbor. Customs officials there were under-paid and under-employed. They had little to do. One day, two of them decided to shake down Craig and Mary and demanded to inspect their boat. As Customs officials they had every right, although they had made only perfunctory inspections of the rest of our boats.

Craig ferried them out in his dinghy. Once on board, they asked questions and poked into closets, all the while suggesting that "this can easily be settled." Craig, a slim but imposing six-foot-three, raised his voice to express his displeasure with the inspection. He had had children, he said, his voice booming, and when his children had angered him, he had killed them. Continuing to shout, Craig gave each of the officials a pack of cigarettes and backed them out of the cabin and into the dinghy. On the way to shore, Craig told more tales of mayhem wrought on the people who'd made him angry, and when they reached the dock, the agents clambered ashore, leaving their cigarettes behind. Grinning as he motored back to his boat, Craig couldn't wait to tell his friends.

In spite of our pleasurable five-day mountain tour, it was easier to leave Sri Lanka than many of the other places we'd enjoyed. Our plan had been to spend a week or so in the Maldive Islands, which have a wonderful reputation for cruising and diving. It was now late March and weather patterns were due to change. In the next two or three weeks, we needed to reach the middle of the Indian Ocean and the Chagos Archipelago and stay there until patterns settled down. The transmission problem had put us behind schedule; we had to give something up. In our rush to leave, we did what long-term provisioning we could at Galle. However, since we expected to be in the Chagos for up to three months, where there is no provisioning of any sort, we needed a stop on the way. Our only option was the island of Addu, the southernmost of the Maldives chain.

Addu is 600 miles on a straight line southwest of Sri Lanka. The first two days went well, with good sailing and fresh fruits and veggies to complement the usual good fare provided by Delwyn and Robert. No traffic, no hassles by fishermen, good wind, easy watches. Then, during a spell of low wind, chugging along under power, the diesel overheated. What now?

There were at least 10 possibilities, so we began to troubleshoot. With little scratching of heads we realized that there wasn't enough water-flow to cool the engine. The probable cause was a worn impeller on the raw (salt) water pump. The pump on *Chandelle* could be reached only through a small opening in the wall by my bunk. The wind was now up and from the south. We were close-hauled, heeling 15° to 20° and bouncing. I had to remove the pump and could get only one arm through the access port. It's a nasty job at the dock, nastier at sea. Knowing this, I had recently changed the impeller; still it was the logical item to inspect first. With the boat's heel, I was half-upside-down. After an hour of disagreeable work, the pump came out. The impeller looked OK, but I installed a new one anyway. After another hour half-upside-down, the pump was back in. It still didn't pump enough water, and my language turned salty.

Possibly the pump's housing was worn, leaving too much clearance. I had a spare, but the supplier hadn't shipped the right model. I had noticed this and had had a machine shop in Sri Lanka make modifications. It was getting dark. We had to do watches all night, so I stopped work. We were hard on the wind. Because the apparent wind was over 20 knots, the wind-generator would keep the batteries up. (Of little use most of the time, the wind-generator paid its way on occasions like this.)

Next morning, still hard on the wind, I got half-upside-down again to pull the old pump out and put the new one in. It didn't fit. The machine shop forgot a step. Robert would have done his share of the work, except that his esophagus sphincter muscle was problematic and prevented him from working upside-down. While I cursed, he thought. Taking parts from the old pump and parts from the new, using the file and appropriate expletives, we produced a working pump—two hours before we had to drop sail and motor into the harbor at Addu.

There is a bumper sticker that says, "A bad day of sailing is better than a good day at the office." After these two days, the office looked good. Golf and gardening looked good. My log says, "Arrived Addu April 3; broke inner forestay; lost staysail cover; radar reflector almost gone (came loose from its mounting on the upper spreader). Many things wet; all very tired." With the hook down and *Chandelle* snug in Addu's well-protected harbor, life and sailing regained their appeal.

Addu is an all-coral island of five or six square miles, with a small diving resort (closed for the season), a tiny beach, and one industry. A clothing company had hired a thousand Sri Lankan girls to work on Addu with the understanding that they (the girls) would be well-looked-after. As far as we could tell, they were. The company housed them in a dormitory, and according to the Muslim and Hindu mores of Sri Lanka, allowed them almost no contact with men.

We saw little of the girls, but did befriend two men, Fritz and Mano. The men were Sri Lankans hired to run the company's industrial kitchen and see that the girls were fed. Fritz and Mano had a number of things that were useful to us, most of all, the plastic containers shaped like jerry cans used to ship cooking oil. Anticipating a need to store more diesel and dinghy fuel, we glommed onto every one they had. With the girls off-limits, social life for Fritz and Mano was nearly nonexistent. We dropped by their office almost every day for advice or just to chat. They clearly enjoyed our company and one night cooked us a fine meal ashore. However, we couldn't reciprocate. Immigration would let us ashore, but would arrest Fritz and Mano if they were caught "leaving the country illegally" to visit our boat.

While we were there, airline service to the island, which brought in most of its supplies, suddenly stopped—whether from a strike or a lack of business. The other supply source, a freighter, was late. When it did arrive, it couldn't unload for days because a small tanker was using the only dock. Fritz and Mano had a crisis. How to feed the girls? They let it be known that they would pay a handsome sum to anyone who brought them a chicken. Typically for that part of the world, the island had a contingent of "wild" chickens. Local youngsters made lots of pocket money reducing the population. The term *free range* seldom had more meaning.

Addu supplied us with diesel fuel and gasoline (both hand-pumped from large storage tanks), bread, bananas, rest, and little else. We bought Fritz and Mano beers in what passed for a bar, then with a dozen jerry cans lashed on deck, we pushed off for the Chagos Archipelago, almost due south. We were close-hauled, but with light winds, calm seas, and everything working, this leg was a delightful contrast to our last.

23

Intermezzo in the Chagos

In Australia I had been introduced to email, the medium that has overwhelmed the world. It was a wonderful expansion of my sparse contacts with family and friends back home, but my initial forays were limited to writing brief notes while sitting in an internet café. With coaching from Robert and Delwyn, I learned to write to a floppy disk on the boat. Now I could write longer notes, massage them beforehand, send the notes in much less time, and archive them. I ask the reader to approach them as a family member or friend who has had no word for some months—and cares. They read in reverse order of events: telling of our arrival at Mayotte, then recapping our experiences in the Chagos. We reached Mayotte three months after leaving Addu, having sailed south to the Chagos, then southwest to Mayotte, which is tucked between Madagascar and Kenya.

June 18, 2000—*Chandelle* Safe and Sound.
Hello and greetings from Mayotte! It's a small picturesque island northwest of Madagascar. Don't be lazy, look it up. Anyway, it's 1,700 miles from the Chagos Archipelago where we have been for the last couple of months. More on that later.
The trip here was spirited. We made it in 11 days, making 179 nautical miles in 24 hours: a *Chandelle* record. Most was great sailing with winds 15-25 knots on a broad reach. As we approached the northern tip of Madagascar, the winds, current, and seas increased. We had winds to 40 knots and above and steep, choppy seas. Nasty. In the lee of Madagascar, the wind died and the water smoothed. We were becalmed for 10 hours. Eventually, the shape of Mayotte appeared one morning, right where it was supposed to be.
We are now anchored in a lovely bay off a small town that the guide says has good facilities. Mayotte is a French resort, so we expect good cheese, good wine, and good provisions (our first source in two-and-a-half months) at a high price. And we have email. We will be here for a couple of weeks, anyway, so let me hear from you.
This is also the first time in two-and-a-half months that I have touched shoes—or my wallet. Those who know me well can imagine my grin on *that*.

The following portions of the email were written in the Chagos, but could not be sent until we arrived in Mayotte.

April 9, 2000

We are in the Chagos Archipelago, which is 5°South, 71°East, 400 miles southwest of India, and 300 miles south of the equator. It is such a unique place that I feel compelled to write about it, and since I now know how to put this on a disk, I may be even wordier than before.

On our trip down here from Addu, we had more wind than we expected and almost made it with two nights at sea. The last night we spent hovering off the coast before making an easy entrance the next day. We are in a group of islands called Peros Banhos. Once a volcano, they are now a circle of idyllic atolls, each with a white sandy beach edged with palm trees. Inside the circle are anchorable depths and shelter from the prevailing southwest to southeast winds. A dozen other cruising boats are sprinkled throughout the area, but there are no inhabitants.

Boats here pick an atoll and use it as a private island. We did that for several days. Then friends talked us into joining them and others by the largest island, which, among other advantages, has a well. Socializing has included two cookouts on shore plus mutual help. We traded tea for powdered eggs.

Boats come here for several reasons. It's a convenient stopover about halfway across the Indian Ocean; the shelter is good, and the fishing is great. It's a perfect place to wait for the monsoon seasons to change. And it's free, almost. A small boat with British sailors appears periodically to collect a small fee. They own the area or have simply declared that they do. The only supplies are fish, if you can catch them. You come with what you will eat for the two or three months of your stay (some stay six months and more). We are now in our banana period, having bought a 75-pound bunch in Addu that came ripe all at once. Discussions among boats are of egg storage, fish preservation, canning, etc., in addition to the usual boat talk. One couple has cruised Japan and eastern Russia. Another has cruised on their 26-foot sailboat for six years. There is only one other American boat.

For the two months we anticipate, it seems like Utopia: no pressures, no expenses, just books to read (I'm on *The Wealth and Poverty of Nations*, by David Landes—a Harvard boy, so he must be right), fish to catch, varnishing, and chats with neighbors. Shall I go for a swim or grease a winch? Decisions, decisions.

May 11, 2000

We have been here for a month. We are in the "Chagos routine." There is a lot to do. Anyone who owns a boat knows that there are always projects. Varnishing is almost done, half the winches have been greased, and several little jobs accomplished that wouldn't get on the list in a normal harbor.

Parkinson's Law is operative; boredom and ennui are not. There is much socializing among boats, with BBQs and potluck picnics on shore. We trade books and CDs, but are under no pressure, no date when we have to leave. When we get tired of one anchoring spot, we move to another. We discovered a great spot by chance in the lee of a small atoll. Good anchoring depth, great snorkeling, and fishing right off the boat. The atoll is a rookery for one or two bird species. One spends most of its time soaring over us. There must be a thousand of them. They form an outline of the thermal, all circling the same way—left—and follow the thermal as it spins off the island.

We eat a lot of fish, catching it late in the day so it isn't too old. We have run out of nothing serious. The banana period is over, potatoes are gone (got wet and spoiled), yet our galley and galleys on other boats still produce great food. We swim every day, use the soap friends brought us months earlier, and rinse with fresh water. To save water, we forego showers. We catch all the rainwater we can and run our water-maker (and diesel) as little as possible.

Sing-Along, Chagos

In spite of being close to the equator, we've had only a few days we considered hot. There is almost always a breeze. Skies are mostly blue, and clouds are mostly fair-weather cumulus. We want more rain showers. We like the water.

We can't communicate out, but we do get U.S.A. Public Radio from a U.S. base on an island about 80 miles from here (Diego Garcia), so we get enough news to keep up with politics and wars.

This place is pretty, and all seems right with the world.

While enjoying this idyllic life of leisure—palm trees waving in the breeze, surf breaking on the reef, yachts swinging gently (mostly) at anchor—a disturbing story has surfaced. You may recall our experience in Borneo up the Kumai River, visiting the orangutan rehabilitation center. It remains a highlight of the trip to have met and played with the animals, however semi-tame they may be. I reported on the battle to keep loggers from encroaching on the park. Things have become worse. One boat anchored here, *Northern Magic*, we have known for some time. The woman, Diane, is a professional writer. She and her family of five had an experience similar to ours while visiting the park, except that toward the end of the visit, she volunteered to help raise money for the enterprise by her writing. The offer was welcomed by the tour guide, one Ashley Lieman. So our friend began to ask questions and request visits to related facilities. She wanted particularly to interview Biruté Galdikas, the Canadian primatologist and one-time protégé of the Leakys (along with Jane Goodall and Dian Fossey).

Galdikas was responsible for starting and managing the rehabilitation center and the supporting organization, Orangutan Foundation International or OFI. I can't go into details, the story is too complicated, but the response to interview requests was bizarre. All such requests were denied. An interview eventually took place over the phone, with Galdikas making vitriolic statements to Diane about everything and everybody. Our friend interviewed over a hundred people, mostly former employees and coworkers of Galdikas. A disturbing picture emerged. It appears that Galdikas has done no scientific work for over 20 years.

She lives not in the camp, where the animals are supposedly being introduced to the wild; instead, she lives in one of the best houses in a town many miles away. She is in league with the loggers who are poaching on the park. People with whom she is associated are exporting orangutans, which is illegal. A former employee was asked to poison a visitor for asking too many questions. The employee declined and left the organization. Several former associates think that Galdikas is only interested in self-aggrandizement, that she has lost any genuine interest in the animals. Many years ago she was on the cover of *National Geographic* magazine. The park and animals are in desperate need of help. Galdikas and the OFI have disappointed many people who are interested in helping.

Since our visit last July, a building in the town of Kumai housing a presentation on the park and the animals was destroyed by marauding men thought to be loggers. A group of scientists who had gone into the park for scientific work were threatened with physical harm by a group of men wielding machetes, presumably loggers. The scientists were forced to leave their camp in minutes and leave all their work behind. Galdikas's bodyguard led the attack. Galdikas was called and asked if her boat (a speedboat) could be used to help with the evacuation. She refused. Right now, the loggers are winning.

I would not know all this, except that Diane and family are here in the anchorage. She asked me to read and comment on a lengthy article she is writing for a Canadian magazine. I have no reason to doubt her word.

Enough of that for now; it's time for my guitar lesson.

May 23, 2000

We are still in the Chagos, although we have moved about 26 miles to another archipelago formed from an ancient volcano and called the Salomon Islands (not to be confused with the Solomon Islands in the South Pacific). The Salomons are a smaller group of six atolls. Each has a white sandy beach and palm trees stirring in the breeze under a perfect sky. These islands offered us better protection and 35 or so more boats for company. Yesterday, Robert caught three large fish, and since our freezer is full, we called on the radio to invite all boats to a beach cookout. Twenty people showed up. A good party.

We've been in the Chagos roughly seven weeks. In addition to fish and lobster, we have harvested coconuts, hearts of palm, lemon grass, papaws, and breadfruit. We have seen fish of every color, shape, and size; manta rays (once, four at the same time); all too many sharks (Robert saw a 14-footer—*that* got everyone out of the water), although the sharks seemed more curious than hungry. The coral is mixed, not the best we've seen. Lots of it is dead, but some spots offer fine snorkeling. Rainy days have filled everyone's water tank. Those without water-makers were getting short. The weather is beginning to change.

We have not been trouble-free. The oven suddenly smoked badly. Fixed that. A fitting on the water-maker broke. Jury-rigged that. Now the cutless bearing is slipping. (This is the bearing that holds the propeller shaft where the shaft goes through the hull.) That's a worry. There is no haul-out facility for several thousand miles.

Our news is sparse but adequate. I miss knowing what is happening to friends and family and look forward to emails when we get to civilization. A few boats are leaving. We plan to leave so that when we approach Madagascar, about three weeks from now, we'll have a full moon. We'll miss this place. It's been a unique experience.—Bob

We left after two more weeks. Weather patterns were changing, bringing more wind from the southeast, instead of the southwest, and more rain. Good friends left for the Seychelles. That had been our plan and would have been wonderful, except that following the coast of East Africa was a much longer trip requiring a more frantic pace, and we had both mechanical and medical worries. I'd been stone deaf in one ear for several weeks and had a growth and sore spot on a leg that was getting worse. Mayotte promised better shops for both boat and body.

To compensate for missing the Seychelles, we planned to stop on the way to Mayotte at a small reef, the Egmont, which was famous for its remoteness, snorkeling, and fishing. We set off in company with another boat, *Beau Soleil,* sailed by a family with a precocious 12-year-old boy named Falcon.

All went well until the first night. I was on watch and noticed that the wind had increased and swung south such that we would be hard on the wind, if we continued on course for the reef. Always attracted to (though not devoted to) the adage, "Gentlemen never sail to weather," I bore off more directly toward Madagascar. Robert replaced me on watch. Finding us now committed to missing the reef, he expressed disappointment in both my decision and my management style. I had never imposed RHIP (rank hath its privileges), so understood his reaction. He wanted to see the reef, and we had abandoned *Beau Soleil.* Over the next several days, we followed their progress by radio. They made the reef, though had a hard time finding it and had to hide behind an island for a day in heavy weather. I still like my decision; I'm not sure Robert has forgiven me.

We were well off the wind and for the first few days had fine sailing: steady winds, occasional showers, ocean current going our way. Watches proceeded, meals appeared, (dishes got washed, that was my job), fish were caught, both GPSs worked and confirmed great progress. As we closed on the northern tip of Madagascar, the winds built—eventually to 40 knots. With no main and a reefed jib, *Chandelle* charged like a racehorse: 7-8 knots was standard. We made sure that Harvey (the autopilot) could handle it. As I said in my Mayotte email, we logged 179 nautical miles in 24 hours.

Great stuff, but winds and seas kept getting stronger. We were tired: tired of the motion and tired of the work required to get food and use the head. The motion made sleep difficult. Somewhere ahead, over the horizon, where shelter in the lee seemed like heaven awaiting, the cape of Madagascar beckoned. Without accurate navigation, such as that provided by GPS, we would have had to give the cape wide birth. We wanted to see the cape and had no interest in sailing an extra mile. We'd been at sea eight days, the wind mostly brisk, the deck in motion under us. Any stable surface would be welcome.

It was essential to reach Madagascar in daylight and preferable to get there in the morning, with the sun at our backs. We controlled boat speed by rolling the jib in and out (the main was down and furled). Every hour or so, the watch used a calculator and pad to determine the speed necessary to get us to the cape at nine o'clock on the appropriate morning, then adjusted the jib to attain that speed. After sunrise on the morning we arrived, only a distant blur showed through the haze. The blur gradually sharpened to a rocky coast with an old, abandoned lighthouse. Crew spirits soared. The promise of calm water was just hours, soon minutes, away.

Also on the horizon was a sail. Radio contact revealed it to be a boat we knew well from the Chagos. Since I'm about to be critical, I won't use the name. The couple on board were friendly, just way under-budgeted and lazy. Their boat was on the verge of collapse. No one wanted to be sailing near them should a disaster occur, like a mast breaking. While the yachting community is as cooperative and helpful as any (far more so than most), these folks took advantage. They accepted parts, supplies, and help, offering little in return. We were happy to see them head down the Madagascar coast, while we headed west to Mayotte.

In 100 yards, the winds went from 40 knots to nothing. In spite of it being three months since we'd refueled, we were OK for fuel and relished the calm of flat seas and the soporific effect of the diesel. Sleep was good again—until we were rudely awakened by a 35-knot gust. We had been warned. The wind, when it hits the coast of Madagascar, goes skyward for miles, then returns to the surface to catch an unwary sailor by surprise. We put up sail and closed on Mayotte after eleven days at sea.

24

The Island of Mayotte and the Race

Here is my email written after a week in Mayotte.

June 25, 2000—Hello Everyone and Greetings from *Chandelle*.
We are in Mayotte and enjoying it. It's a small island, about 100 miles west of the north point of Madagascar. Volcanic in origin, Mayotte is surrounded by a reef, which provides a fine lagoon of quiet waters. The anchorage is well-protected and good-holding. The environment on shore is agreeable and relatively modern. The women, particularly, wear colorful robes and sometimes a mud mask, much as Western women wear lipstick.

We are always doing projects, so we have to deal with shops and services. Not easy. Everything is spread out and few people speak English. My French is nonexistent. Everyone tries to be helpful, but communicating even a mildly complex idea is a struggle—sometimes amusing, sometimes disastrous.

We met the director of the French Telecom office. In addition to being hugely helpful, he invited all his English-speaking friends (three) and us for dinner. He was leaving Mayotte for another job so his employees were giving him a going-away picnic. We went to that and experienced a native soiree. It was much like a picnic at home: chicken parts over an open fire and salad. He had a car and took us on a tour of the island. It is spectacular country: fertile and uncrowded and ripe for change. Sixty percent of the population is under age 20.

About a week ago there was a referendum on whether or not to strengthen ties with France and gain the attendant economic and administrative benefits. Not an easy choice because it meant converting to French law. Most of Mayotte's population is Islamic, and Islam—here, at least—encourages many wives (up to four, anyway). There were other issues fueling bitter opposition, but the vote approved the move toward France.

Every Bastille Day, Mayotte holds a regatta. We have been encouraged to enter and are able to interrupt our projects. Of the 50 or 60 other boats in the harbor, 31 have signed up for the race and several look fast. We are the only American boat. We cleaned the bottom, stowed the things that walk out of place in a harbor, secured a friend for additional crew, and added *Chandelle* to the race list. With our rail festooned in BBQ and fishing gear and our lockers full of cans and etceteras, we didn't consider ourselves competitive. Other boats had off-loaded gear, including anchors and chain, and had *practiced*.

The day of the regatta was beautiful, with light winds and calm seas. I was nervous. Not knowing how to shout in French for buoy room or right-of-way ("Starboard!"), I decided to be conservative. We timed the start well and the boat felt good. Halfway to the weather mark, I looked back and the only boat close to us was a Hobie Cat. We don't count that.

We were first around the weather mark, followed by two boats that we knew had practiced. They set spinnakers and began to close on us. We thought the leg too short to risk a chute. We hadn't set it in six months. A Jeanneau 42 passed us at a jibe mark. We cut behind, took his wind, and his chute collapsed. Delwyn, likely the kindest person I've known, thought the maneuver unsportsmanlike. Robert and I explained that sailing races are vicious.

We passed the Jeanneau and never lost the lead. On a long leg, we had two boats close behind. Both had their spinnakers set, so we had to set ours. Suddenly, we had to jibe it. We—actually Robert—succeeded.

The race chart was confusing as to which of two buoys was the downwind mark. I got on the radio and asked for clarification but received no response. Every boat in the race would have heard me. Making a good guess by covering the Jeanneau, we rounded the leeward mark a few lengths ahead. The Jeanneau, still within striking distance, started a tacking duel, but we won on every tack and finished seven minutes in the lead after four-and-a-half hours.

There was lots of applause and tooting of horns. Great fun, and far and away the prettiest course I have ever raced: many islands to round, wind shadows and currents to consider, many buoys to find. In all respects, this was a spectacular day. At an after-race party, we received many congratulations; still, I think the French egos were damaged to have a bloody Yank steal the show. Every boat got a prize. I got a free ride in an ultra-light and plan to go tomorrow. (If you got this, I survived.)

I've run on too much about the race, but it's hard to get us on any other subject right now.

Projects are getting done, notably a new inner forestay (the old one broke on the way to Addu) and a re-hang of the porthole windows (the hinges were rusting out). Having heard many fine things about cruising in Madagascar, we want to head east. Since occasionally someone expresses genuine interest in our welfare and safety (mostly family), let me explain our plan. We will sail in about a week for the two- to three-day trip to Madagascar, then cruise the northwest coast for about three months. Sometime in late October, we'll head across the Mozambique Channel, spend relatively little time on the Mozambique coast, and arrive in Richard's Bay near Durban, South Africa, sometime in November. Note that Madagascar and Mozambique are poor countries. Phones don't work, and mail is a disaster. Postal employees steam, then sell the stamps off letters. Email may be nonexistent, and if so, communication from us will be as well. Rest assured, we will probably survive.

Thanks to those who sent me email; boo to those who didn't.

We will be here for only a few more days, so messages you send me after that may get lost.

We look forward to the trip ahead. We also look forward to South Africa, where at least some things are First World, or so we're told.—Love and hugs to everyone, Bob

We had planned to stay in Mayotte three weeks and stayed seven. An adventure not reported in the email was my trip to Réunion Island. By the time we reached Mayotte, my one-ear deafness and leg-sore were part of my life. They were a major reason for coming to Mayotte. After we arrived, I climbed up a steep hill in heat over 90°F to a new hospital building—the kind of facility Mayotte's association with France provided. Such was not available in the neighboring Comoros Islands. I was directed to an Eye, Ear, Nose, and Throat clinic. The doctor had a big smile, spoke excellent English, and brandished a terrifyingly long needle, which he proceeded to stick in my ear. One "thwooop" of suction and I could hear perfectly. It had been wax all along.

Next stop was the General Practice clinic. The waiting room was large, poorly lit, and filled with about 20 natives, mostly women with babies. It was close to noon and I suspect most had been waiting since the clinic opened, probably 8:00 a.m. I would be there many hours. All the benches were filled, so the ladies directed me to stand by a door. Soon a patient came out of the door, followed by the nurse looking for the next patient. I glanced around the room to see who that might be and saw all the ladies directing me to enter. I looked around again. All were smiling, gesturing for me to go. I protested, but it was unanimous. I never understood why.

The doctor, French like the other, was in Mayotte for the excellent clinical experience. He seemed to like having a non-native body to scrutinize. Shortly, however, he pronounced my sore leg beyond Mayotte's medical expertise. I should go to either South Africa or Réunion Island, and yes, I should: the sore was serious. Well, that would affect our plans.

On the walk up to the hospital, I had noticed a travel agent's office, which, after profound thanks to the doctor and again to the ladies who had ushered me in, became my next stop. Réunion Island was closer and cheaper than South Africa. There was a direct flight, so on the spot, I booked a seat two days hence, with two days in a moderately priced hotel. The agent warned me that I would find Réunion more expensive than Mayotte.

Robert and Delwyn took the news well—extremely well. I think they enjoyed having time on the boat without the captain.

I went off to Réunion, on the opposite side of Madagascar from Mayotte. Bright sun hid the effects of slash-and-burn farming, making the mountains of Madagascar look their best. The evening sun revealed Réunion as an old and huge volcano. Wealthier than Mayotte, with a population in the hundreds of thousands, Réunion had high-rise buildings, high-end cars, and good medical facilities. If I survived the doctor, I wanted to explore.

I had envisioned getting off the plane and asking a taxi driver to take me to a dermatologist. Then I remembered that Pierre, the manager of the Telecom office, was from Réunion. Of course he'd help. With a phone call or two (free, because he worked for the phone company), he found an English-speaking doctor and likely the best one on Réunion.

My plane arrived late in the day, so my appointment was first thing the next morning. The doctor was charming, fluent in English, and had just returned from meetings in the U.S. of the American Dermatological Society, of which he was a member. I couldn't have asked for better. He nipped off the growth and said that while he was reasonably sure that it was not serious, he would send it to a lab. He did, and faxed me days later that all was well.

Now I needed a one-day tour. The hotel found me the perfect one. Réunion had a volcano that was dramatic and active at the time, though viable as a tourist attraction only in good weather. That day it was socked in. The alternative was the ancient caldera where a village nestled among towering peaks, and tourists—busses of them—swarmed like bees to the hive. It was worth the visit. The sun was shining and paths to lookouts offered great walks and great photography. Also on the tour was a vanilla farm. Vanilla is the main export of Réunion, and the aroma permeating every phase of production persuaded me to buy a bottle of vanilla liqueur. (Later, it embellished many a dessert aboard *Chandelle*.) Also on the tour were a butterfly farm with live butterflies and a museum with pinned ones. Both were fascinating and attractive, as was the guide. She was cute.

We left Mayotte after one false start. The day we picked to leave was blustery. While we were tacking out of a narrow channel, a fitting on the backstay caught the mainsail and made a small tear. Back to the harbor we went. The mom on *Beau Soleil*, had sail-repair equipment and the skill to use it. (They were speaking to us again, although we had abandoned them after leaving the Chagos.) With all hands from both boats, we got the main off the boom, into the dink, on shore, and up a hill to the yacht club, where there was a sort of table and enough electric power—barely, it kept dying—to run the sewing machine. Repair made, we folded the sail, hauled it down the hill, dumped it in the dink, motored back to the boat, and put the sail back on. Just another day in the cruising life.

Our second try at leaving Mayotte went well, although most of the time we motored. We arrived at Madagascar at night and had to find our way into the harbor by radar and the guidance by radio of a yachtie already there. A full moon made it easier. Here, we entered a different world.

25

Madagascar and Its Villages

The following email was written the day after arriving in Richard's Bay, South Africa. Read it from the viewpoint of family who had heard nothing from me in three months.

October 14, 2001 (my birthday)—Greetings from South Africa.

Chandelle and crew made it in good shape, and what a finale. During the last 24 hours of our 10-day trip from Madagascar, the winds built to 30 knots and swung around right behind us. During the night we had a full moon, providing great visibility, and during the final day, a cloudless sky. With the Number 3 jib and one reef in the main, we were wung out. Surfing down a wave, we saw 12.8 on the knot meter and 10 knots on GPS, both records. Not bad for a 40-foot boat.

There were lots of porpoise and flying fish, and to top it off, we had the second of two whale sightings a few hours before landfall. It was a thrilling end to a leg fraught with problems.

We left a quiet harbor near the westernmost point on Madagascar after a final round of gift-giving to local villages. We had supplies we knew we'd never use, and we knew the locals needed all the help they could get. As we pulled out of the pass, about a dozen children ran down the beach waving and dancing. It was heartwarming.

Ahead of us were 1,100 challenging miles. I was nervous.

Our first day was easy, downwind sailing. Then the wind died and we had a strong current against us, such that at one point, under full power, we were making only 2.8 knots over the bottom. This was not good. We hadn't taken on fuel for two months and were low. The Mozambique Channel is known for a strong, favorable current. The charts showed where it was supposed to be, but we couldn't find it. Eventually the wind picked up, then picked up more, to 35 knots. We were heavily reefed, hard on the wind, and making good progress, but sleep, for me at least, was impossible.

When we found the favorable current, the wind was blowing from the opposite direction, and disproportional to its strength, it kicked up a short, choppy sea. Under these conditions, the book says, "Heave-to"—bring the boat to a standstill by putting the sails and rudder in opposition.

Thirty-five knots of wind is not usually dangerous, but with the sails in this unusual position, the wind formed a vortex in the slot between main and jib. The whole rig was shaking violently and would come down. We had to do something. We dropped the main and noticed the instantaneous comparative calm. With just the jib sheeted to weather, the calm created was astounding. We had just learned more about sailing. With the boat effectively stopped, all hands took 12 hours of welcome rest. We were blown back 20 miles, but it was worth it.

Getting underway again, we couldn't start the diesel. It would turn over but not catch, yet had given no hint of trouble. It passed all the tests we could give it at sea. No luck. The wind-generator and solar panels would support the batteries, but could not run everything. We had to choose between autopilot and fridge. In the freezer was a 35-pound Dorado that Robert had coaxed over the rail, so we chose to hand-steer. While hand-steering, we enjoyed the sleigh ride and record speeds I mentioned above. We couldn't sail to a dock in a big harbor, so we had to call for a tow—an ignominious ending to a trip for a captain. The local search-and-rescue came out to greet us. All volunteers, they did a superb job of bringing us in. They will get a large contribution from me.

We are now in Richard's Bay, about 60 miles north of Durban. We are delighted to be here. Things work. We are back to civilization with movies, ice cream, and services, e.g., for the diesel.

(Having related my elation at safe arrival in South Africa, I include here the email I wrote much as we experienced things in the preceding three months.)

August 18, 2001

We entered Madagascar at a place called Russian Bay, so named because a hundred years ago, when a Russian warship was abandoned by its government, the sailors beached the ship and went native. Almost totally enclosed, with few native settlements, the bay is a favorite yachtie hangout. A friend was having a birthday party on shore, and eight yachts showed up for pot luck, chit-chat, and games.

Lest ye landlubbers think this life is all indolence and parties, shortly after the socializing above, we went with two other boats we knew well to another isolated bay, where there was no native village. We all had projects. One of *Chandelle*'s spreaders had started to bend. We had some steel stock with which to reinforce it, but had to borrow a drill from one of the other boats. That boat had a weak forestay. They had a spare, but it took six of us to help them make the switch. The third boat needed a major sail repair and was short of thread. We had plenty. Other chores included laundry, cleaning, and general fixing-up. Doing this work in such a wild and beautiful setting is cruising at its classic best.

We went through the check-in procedure for Madagascar in a town called Hellville (named after an early administrator, not someone's evaluation). We had been in the country illegally for several days, but Madagascar hasn't a viable Navy or Coast Guard, so we checked in at our convenience. We had been warned that officials looking for a handout made illegal demands of yachties, but we had no trouble.

With repairs and parties out of the way (for awhile), it was time to go exploring. We sailed north to the small island of Tsara Bajina, which had a tasteful resort. During a walk around, we stuck our heads in the lounge and there was television, in English, showing live cricket between South Africa and Australia. I was in the company of four Aussies and one resort employee from South Africa. No one moved until the game was over. (South Africa won.) The game is a mystery to an American, but it was exciting to get a glimpse of the real world out there. We hadn't seen TV in English since leaving Darwin, Australia.

Tsara Bajina was worth a stop, though the anchorage was small. We had to move three times during the night because the wind kept swinging around forcing us too close to the rocky shore. One such night was enough; we went on to the next island, Mitsio. Our chart was based on 125-year-old surveys and lacked detail. Also, the water was less clear than we were used to. Consequently, we had close calls with the bottom. We made it, and the harbor we found was delightful. Enterprising young men from one of the two small villages took our T-shirts in trade for lobsters and pawpaws. We spent two nights there, permitting a long walk ashore, then moved back south to the relative sophistication of Hellville. As I write, Robert and Delwyn are off for a few days to travel on land, while I guard the boat. Then we will switch.

Time for some reactions to this country. With its long geologic separation from Africa and Gondwanaland, Madagascar developed unique flora and fauna. Some still exist. Homo sapiens is the newcomer. He is doing his usual damage. Slash-and-burn farming has destroyed 80 percent of the forest, and all the rivers run red with erosion. He has not treated himself well, either. An early queen had 600 missionaries thrown off a cliff. The French assumed control of the island and to quell an uprising, hired Senegalese mercenaries. They happily murdered 80,000 natives. That was in 1947. This is only part of Madagascar's dark history, so it is surprising to find that most natives are friendly and helpful.

In Hellville itself, there is crime, although not to the person. At night when we go to town, we clear the deck of all loose items. Outboard motors are a favorite of thieves. Outside Hellville and in the remote villages, crime is low. There, natives in their canoes keep a respectful distance from the boat until called over. However, they are no pushovers at bargaining. They know a quality T-shirt.

The country is one of the poorest in the world. We are back to dugout canoes and grass huts: colorful and quaint for us, poverty for them. They are not as well-dressed as the folks in Mayotte, except for a few young girls who are remarkably well-dressed. My curiosity piqued, I considered making a thorough investigation of this phenomenon.

In the outlying villages, natives are glad for gifts of empty cans and bottles and even for empty beer cans, from which we assume they make fishing lures. The fishing here is excellent, for them and for us. They look well-fed on fish, rice, and manioc. Many live in grass huts in small villages sprinkled around the bays and islands. There are no roads; transportation is by dugout canoe. Separating their life from that of the Stone Age are the machete, metal cooking pots, and a few plastic bottles for carrying water. The natives seem cheerful and content. With no electric power and hence no TV, they seem only vaguely aware of their circumstances compared to the rest of the world. In towns where power and TV do exist, one senses the desire for money and envy toward the Westerner.

One circumnavigator I talked to thinks this coast offers the best cruising in the world. I may agree. There are many islands, many harbors. This time of year, the weather is dry and the air is clear. Most mornings, an offshore breeze sends the native boats out to fish and the few yachties out to sail. The wind dies around midday, then an onshore breeze fills in to bring everyone home again. It's been this way for hundreds of years and is reflected in the native boat design: simple square rigs—great for photos.

Pirogue, Madagascar

We are meeting boats from South Africa. This is their cruising ground. And since South Africa is our next destination, we collect all the advice we can

Madagascar and Its Villages   137

on how to proceed. Several readers have emailed reports on murderous weather and pirates in the Mozambique Channel. The latter is discussed frequently among us yachties. Your concern is appreciated, but the channel must be crossed. Many boats make the trip, and we will probably survive. (If you're reading this, we did.)

Now it was my turn to travel inland while Robert and Delwyn guarded the boat. I flew north to a town called Diego Suarez, a relatively large town near the North Cape. The town itself was depressing: hot, dry, nearly treeless, with dirty concrete buildings. The area was nearly treeless, too, having been subjected to slash-and-burn farming for the last 50 years. Why did I go there? Nearby is the most visited park in Madagascar, home to many unique species. I set off with a guide, a driver, and another tourist. We saw three species of lemur as well as chameleons, geckos, mongoose, and birds (one unique to that park) plus unusual flora and geologic formations. We camped in the forest and slept in tents. The driver was a good cook; the guide was knowledgeable in all areas, including plants the natives use for medicinal purposes. Few here have the money to see Western-trained doctors or buy the medicines they might prescribe.

Around South Africa

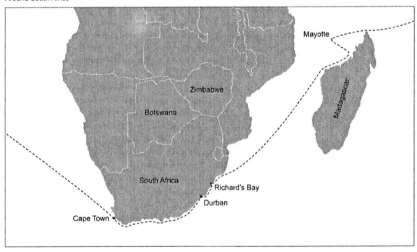

I'm now back on the boat and we have officially checked out of the country. We won't actually leave yet; there is more we want to see. Officials have no effective patrol boats, so we are not concerned about legalities. As I write, we are in a gorgeous spot with good protection from weather.

The last few weeks have been great. Day sails with good winds on flat seas, alternating with lay days in beautiful bays and visits to and from the many local villages. We brought the natives gifts of empty cans and bottles, old clothing, soap, and food—mostly canned goods. In return, they gave us bananas, fish, lobster, crab, honey, and profound gratitude.

We saw a single family living alone by a small spring: father, 25; mother, 20; children of eight, six, four, and one. Put some arithmetic to that. She had her first child at 12. How many children will they have? What kind of future is there for them and for Madagascar?

Over the past year we have taken a peek at how a billion or so people live. In the main, they are happy, but the contrast with our Western experience is breathtaking. Madagascar is the poorest society we have visited. Forests are toppled for export to meet the demands of foreign institutions (e.g., the World Bank) for interest payments on loans. Schools and medical clinics are closed. The future for Madagascar looks bleak.

Village Teacher, Madagascar

It is now October 3, and we are preparing to sail for South Africa. We are about to leave the Third World, where people use a tiny portion of the earth's assets, for the First World—at least that part of South Africa that is First World—where people are using up the earth's assets in a hurry. We have to admit that we are looking forward to being where stuff is available and things work.

Yes, we are apprehensive about crossing the Mozambique Channel, but we talk to other boats doing the same thing, and we are preparing as well as we know how. Weather forecasting is good, even if the weather may not be. We'll be OK.—Bob

26

South Africa and a Return to Civilization

After our dramatic arrival, we slipped comfortably into a completely new life in Richard's Bay. With *Chandelle* secured to a concrete wall, where the tide range was two feet and motion was unknown, we concentrated on our sick diesel. What to do? Again, the answer was to draw on Robert's experience in his youth. We borrowed from a machine shop the test gear we needed to find the basic problem. As we suspected, it was lack of compression. We had run the diesel too much just charging batteries, and the resulting poor combustion had gummed up the rings and valves. The diesel failed one day from civilization. It could have failed in Madagascar or the Chagos. We were lucky.

The book says to run the diesel in gear when charging batteries, even at the dock. I have seen boats straining at their dock lines, but rarely. I never did it. When at anchor, which had been our norm for the previous six months, I could have raised the anchor and charged around the harbor (a pun there?) or put the gear in reverse and tugged on the anchor line. That would have taken courage. I've never seen anyone do that.

The engine needed a major overhaul. How? There was a local diesel mechanic who worked on yachts. His reputation was terrible. He did nothing on time, and what he did, didn't work. Robert stuck up his hand again, and again I chose his diligence over other options. This would be a big project. It seemed only fair to pay him what I'd have paid a local mechanic. So we bought tools, a fan (soon it would be uncomfortably hot) and rented a small office that we could lock. Parts big and small emerged from *Chandelle*'s engine room. Finally, with it lightened sufficiently to be supported by the boom and topping lift and with the encouragement of neighbors, we struggled the engine block onto the dock. With carts and wheelbarrows, we moved everything to the shop. Robert disassembled and cleaned, while I scoured the area for parts and advice and learned about clearances for pistons, rings, and crankshafts. Parts came in from Australia and the U.S., and slowly the engine reappeared.

That which came out in parts had to go back in whole, and now the diesel was too heavy for the boom-and-topping-lift rig. We needed a crane. Shopping around, I found a family operation that had what we wanted. However, right in the middle of the overhaul, the dock master demanded that I move from our comfortable spot on the main dock to a slip where a crane could not possibly reach us. He was unsympathetic, but by pleading and cajoling I put him off a day at a time. When the crane finally arrived, it was not the small one I had ordered; it was a monster that could have picked up the whole boat or a house. The small crane was booked that day. However, since they charged me at the small crane's rate, all was well. Down the hatch went the diesel, and with coaxing, Robert got it to run.

While all this was going on, we observed South Africa and enjoyed civilization. I bought a 1990 Honda sedan that was useful for chasing parts and visiting local game parks. With the car came advice from locals about the crime rate. Carjacking was frequent and serious and occasionally resulted in murder. "Keep all doors locked and never pick up a rider," was the universal advice. Although we had no trouble, we talked with locals who had been car-jacked and whose neighbors had been shot in a car theft.

Nevertheless, the countryside was beautiful, the game parks fascinating, a trip to the Drackenberg Mountains spectacular and affordable. The dollar bought 12 rand. The first-class hotel in the mountains cost $20 a day, including three excellent meals. The elderly among us (like me) considered using it as a retirement home. Even with the cost of a nurse, it would be cheaper than a U.S. nursing home and vastly more enjoyable.

I had expected to be taken with South Africa and I was. Not so much that it was or is a perfect place. Along with the rest of Africa, it has crushing problems, but it was and is fascinating to see up close and from the local perspective, instead of through the filter of the U.S. press. My extended stays in New Zealand and Australia had been wonderful. Why not extend my stay here? Fine for me, but Robert and Delwyn would move on. They'd had no income for two years, and while the cruising life in the areas we had been was as inexpensive as it gets, their youth, energy, and family pressures made their departure inevitable.

It was time for other reasons also. We got along well almost all the time. Their love of adventure, the outdoors, and wildlife; their ease in making friends; their cooking, fishing, mechanical, and medical skills made it hard to imagine better crew. There are many horror stories about sailors picking up crew. Many turn out to be incompetent, some are alcoholics, others are thieves. Robert and Delwyn were none of these. To this day I thank whatever gods there be for my good fortune.

That said, we were different in age and interests. After two years, the differences began to tell. When they were away, I played Berlioz; when I was away, they played Rock. Books I found intriguing, they did not. They had strong religious beliefs; I do not. None of these things mattered along the way. We had plenty to talk about and stayed off sensitive issues. My logic for finding a couple as crew had paid off handsomely. They were totally supportive of each other. If I teased one, the other got back at me. If we went ashore on a deserted atoll, I walked one way, they the other, for some alone-time. It worked well, but two years was enough. We found a boat going their way captained by an Australian so they could talk about rugby and cricket in Australian. With encouraging words over lunch and a final hug, we said good-bye. Emails keep us up to date. I'm delighted to report that they are doing brilliantly: running a successful business and looking for a boat to buy.

Now I had *Chandelle* to myself again, and I could make just the sort of mess I wanted. I had Mozart and Beethoven for company and good friends on other boats. There was much boat work to do. Some things were worn out and I had many ideas for improvements. A strange guy ran a welding shop at the dock. He was not personable and not communicative, but his welding was excellent. I gave him lots of work.

Someone put up signs around the dock inviting people to a party at a nearby home. I recognized the name as that of a local ham radio operator whom we had talked to and listened to on our trip to South Africa. His was one of those calm voices so welcome at sea when the winds are up, blowing from the wrong direction, and it's raining. His weather information was good and his reassurance that "this too shall pass" raised morale until pass it did. The party seemed like a good chance to meet locals who were not shop owners.

Since I had a car, I offered a charming couple, Tad and Joyce, from the s/v *Lyric* a ride in exchange for their company. We agreed to make a side trip to the Drackenberg Mountains, partly to see the mountains and partly to hear the Drackenberg Boys Choir—one of the best in the world. Both were well worth the visit, and the lodge where we stayed was not only first-class, it cost only $25 a day, including meals. When the swimming pool got too cold for swimmers, baboons took over. They mimicked the tourists. Their whoops and hollers were so human-like it was embarrassing. Are we really that silly?

Then we went to the ham's party. I mention it because of the story he told, which provides insight into the problems of South Africa and perhaps of Africa generally. Now retired, the ham had been a farmer. At one time he'd had some 300 employees—black, of course—with whom he was on good terms. He treated them well. Once, some of them asked why his corn grew so much better than theirs. He guessed that he had access to better seeds and gave them some. Later, they told him how happy they were and how much better their corn grew that season. At the next planting season he asked who wanted more seeds. No one did. No one explained. They all avoided the subject. A few weeks later, they told him that their lives had been threatened. They had been accused of witchcraft, of pulling all the growing energy from the surrounding area to their own corn for their own selfish ends.

High on our pinnacle of wisdom it's easy for us to be critical, but what about all those in our supposedly sophisticated society who believe in flying saucers, homeopathy, and astrology? In Africa, education could eventually counter such irrational beliefs (though education has worked imperfectly in the U.S.), but in a typical family here, the parents are out working—or at least out—and education is left to Granny, who imparts to the young longstanding ideas. Progress may be slow.

Chandelle needed a bottom-to-top paint job, and the only place with a good reputation was in Durban, about 90 miles down the coast. Ninety miles is too long to do in one day from sunrise to sunset, and I wanted to avoid at all costs entering a strange harbor at night. When I discussed my dilemma at the local bar, two healthy-looking guys came over and volunteered to go along. I didn't know either of them. Why did they want to do this? They said they were hired to fix up the tug they were working on and were bored. They wanted a change. That seemed reasonable, and since they were my only option, I took a chance. In a few days an acceptable weather window appeared, and at 2:00 a.m., we set off. One of them slept most of the way; the other didn't sleep at all. We had rain showers (not forecast) and less wind than promised. Still, we made it in good time. At the dock in Durban, I put them on a bus back to Richard's Bay.

One more leg of the trip was behind me, and now I had another community to sort out. The dock had no shore power. A contractor hired to do the job, pocketed the money and left town. There was no more money available, so no shore power. Running the diesel to keep up the batteries to run the fridge was what had caused trouble before. There were three good restaurants right at the dock. For $4 or $5, I could have a good meal with a glass of wine. Why cook?

Durban was different from Richard's Bay. There was more poverty and a different ethnic mix, dominated by Indians and blacks. During the day streets and shops were crowded: no problem. At night, they were dangerous.

My goal was to get the boat painted, so with appointments made, I motored up a harbor tributary into a slip. There the boat was hauled and put up on blocks. This was where I lived for two months.

I took a short trip, and on my return, wrote the following email.

> April 15, 2001—Greetings Everyone.
> I've just come back from another island. It was disappointing in some ways: no clear waters, no colorful fish to see and eat, no white sandy beaches under palm trees waving in the tropical breeze, no tropical breeze. It was freezing when I was there. The natives were diverse and prosperous. They seemed to do well selling trinkets to tourists and to each other.
> One thing puzzled me. Many of the more prosperous people, looking worried, disappeared in the early morning into huge buildings only to reappear late in the day looking worried and tired. There was no apparent production—no baskets, no canoes—just a few bails of scrap paper.
> However, I've gained many wonderful friends among the natives. I miss them already; some I miss a great deal. I must go there more often. (One could conclude that I'm thinking more and more about home.)
> As I write, *Chandelle* and I are on the hard (dry dock) in a down-at-the-mouth yard near Durban. I have a long list of projects. Labor rates being what they are, I can afford to get a lot done here. We yachties often comment on how much of the time we are fixing stuff. It's like redecorating an apartment every few months.
> Close friends of mine here visited the neighboring country of Swaziland. It is a small country, actually a kingdom, by the northeast corner of South Africa next to Mozambique. It is essentially black and may be typical of many African countries. The average woman has six to eight children, but the population is declining because of AIDS. Five years ago, 20 percent of women attending a prenatal clinic were HIV-positive. In July 1999, the number was 35 percent; now it is 40 percent. Sixty percent of babies born to HIV-positive women live less than three years. Caesarean births and bottle-feeding could greatly reduce the mortality rate, but there is no money for milk powder, no access to clean water for drinking, and no refrigeration. Babies die of malnutrition, gastroenteritis, and cholera, of which there is currently an epidemic.
> In a hospital my friends visited, 90 percent of all patients were HIV-positive; 95 percent of TB patients were HIV-positive. The average life expectancy of HIV-positive patients is seven to eight years, and during this time a man may infect 25 other people. Thirty percent of the general population is known to be HIV-positive. The real figure is likely much higher.

Although the government of Swaziland has a massive education program, behavior is not changing. Everyone has multiple partners. Women have no power to refuse sex or to insist on condoms. Men like dry sex, for which paper and chemicals are put in the vagina (don't ask me to explain that one). That causes lacerations and bleeding, hence infection.

One teacher told my friends that four years ago only three or four children in her class knew of anyone who had died of AIDS. Last month, at the same question, all children knew several. Years ago school fees were waived for AIDS orphans. Now there are so many orphans, the kids have to leave school. A local furniture manufacturer used to make coffins on the side; now he makes only coffins. There is plenty of used furniture available.

The numbers in other areas of South Africa are probably similar, but until recently, the South African government declared that HIV doesn't lead to AIDS. On April 5, 2001, following a study that cost 2 million rand, the government finally announced that AIDS is a result of HIV. A month before, an activist had said, "AIDS will disappear, if testing blood for HIV is outlawed." AIDS is the number-one cause of death in prisons; 3,000 prisoners are known to be HIV-positive. One province alone reported over 6,000 rapes or attempted rapes. Thirty-nine percent of young blacks want to emigrate; 60 percent of young whites want to emigrate. Fifty-five police have been killed so far this year. Schools often have 100 children in a class. I could go on. Where will this lead?

On a lighter note, the following is an ad for a night club on the local radio: "Come visit the ACME club. Come not only to enjoy our comely young ladies, but to help them to their goals. Doris dances to make money to further her education. Alice dances to finance her young son's periodontal work. Janice dances to pay for a wheelchair for her invalid mother. Maria dances to pay for much-needed breast-reduction surgery. We urge that you attend before Maria goes under the knife."

As you can imagine, this ad got mixed reviews. After a few weeks, it was taken off the air. What effect it had on the club's business, I'll never know.

Enough for now. I would love to hear from any and all.—Bob

Being on the hard is agony. Writing interestingly about it is daunting and reading about it, likely worse. Yet unique things happened while I was in the yard, so I beg one paragraph of your time. At 7:30 the first morning, I awoke to hear six young men scratching their nails across a blackboard. That's what it sounded like. They were using razor-blade scrapers on the outside of the hull. The noise was awful, and the whole hull had to be scraped. That lasted a week. Mast and boom came off with a crane. All fittings came off the deck. The boat looked forlorn.

Life would have been intolerable without the tiny restaurant that fed the yard workers lunch and fed dinner to the several yachties whose boats were going through processes similar to mine. An interesting couple ran the Greasy Spoon, as they called it. They were well-educated, though had made bad business decisions (never explained) and were eking out a living this way. He defended the Afrikaner apartheid policies. Most yachties took the other side, which made for spirited conversations. The food was uninspired, but the social life around it made up for that. A local character, who lived on a boat there, had been an operative for the former South African government's equivalent of the CIA. He had led a military attack on the Seychelles, fingered some highly-placed politicians in other governments as drug dealers, and was now an arms dealer. He showed me emails from someone who needed a buyer for a stash of arms and ammunition now out of U.S. jurisdiction in Haiti. I'm convinced that the story was genuine.

Eventually, the boat got back together and into the water.

June 7, 2001—Greetings Everyone.
Time for another "Letter from South Africa."

Chandelle is back in the water after two months on the hard. High time. Drawers and doors fit again, and I don't have to climb a ladder every time I go aboard. Many things got done and she looks great. I could and did hire semi-skilled labor (read blacks)—men in their 20s who were willing workers, cheerful, and adequately skilled in sanding and painting—for about $9 a day.

I am now in Durban at a yacht club, having revised the former plan, which was to go back to Richard's Bay. I have met interesting people here, including several musicians in the symphony orchestra, the last professional orchestra in South Africa. A couple on another boat have musical interests similar to mine and we have gone to four concerts and a birthday party for a trumpeter. There are other theater and art activities here, whereas Richard's Bay is a comparative vacuum. During the last several years I have been confined to CDs, borrowing movies from other yachts, and occasionally attending events back home in New York. OK, this orchestra is not world-class, but my longing for music is satisfied, and it's fun to know several of the performers. It's like knowing members of a theater group at home.

Soon I board a plane for Nairobi, Kenya, to join a safari organized by friends from Beantown (that's Boston). I will report.

More on the flavor of South Africa. In my last letter, which described the AIDS crisis sweeping this continent, I should have included a description of the makeup of South Africa. There are four basic groups: white Europeans, mostly Dutch and English; Indians, imported 100 years ago to cut sugar cane; the so-called "colored," descendants of natives and European sailors (conventional wisdom had it that only ordinary sailors would do such a thing, now it is universally agreed that the officer class was well-represented); and blacks, the real natives. There is no love between the Afrikaner and the English, and there is as much hatred between black tribes as there is black to white.

Because mores and history are different among these groups, the horrendous HIV statistics I related about the neighboring Kingdom of Swaziland likely apply only to the blacks in South Africa. Accurate local statistics are hard to come by. The government wouldn't publish crime numbers for two years—ostensibly because they were unreliable, probably because they were bad. President Mbeki still won't say that HIV and AIDS are related, so any numbers on this subject are suspect.

So far, Mbeki has refused to criticize Robert Mugabe of Zimbabwe and Mugabe's policies, which are devastating that country. White farmers are run off their property; blacks take over who won't use modern farming methods, and the country is now short on food. Before, Zimbabwe was a food exporter.

Hundreds of South African farmers have been murdered, supposedly because land reform was too slow. The government here is in over its head: simply not competent. Mbeki is overwhelmed and much of the rest are also corrupt. The national minister of education would not enter her office for three months because someone had put a hex on it. At the same time, in Richard's Bay, private (read white) schools teach children that blacks are descended from apes, while whites are descended from God. So much for breaking down barriers.

There are bright spots. The country is beautiful and has many natural resources, including the game parks and animals. Tourism is big business here. The press appears free and regularly heaps vituperation on the government, president, and others. As I write, alleged corruption in a major purchase of military hardware is getting national attention. After spending millions on arms, officials suddenly "found" a Mercedes Benz in their driveway. Government officials at all levels are in jail. Perhaps lessons are being learned. A radio talk show, not like any I have heard in the States, is hosted by a black of obvious competence. He has people of all types on his show and also takes call-ins. The show has its percentage of people who are whacko, but also many thoughtful people. Businessmen, doctors, lawyers, and others call in with worthwhile points of view. While there is a large brain-drain, many people are working incredibly hard to make this country work. I wish them success.

Now, I need to unburden myself. I have been the only American in the boatyard and now on the dock. I mix regularly with people from all over the world and have had many interesting discussions on many topics. I am regularly asked to comment on U.S. policies and actions. After the 2000 elections, I was told by friends at home that I should be happy to have a Republican in the White House; yet from here, this guy looks like a disaster. His policies are at odds with reality. I'm in a continent in desperate need of family planning, which new U.S. policy has just made more difficult.

Also, I can find no justification for this missile-shield thing that is supposed to protect us from weapons launched a world away. It looks like pap to the military-industrial complex about which President Eisenhower warned us. The newspaper here characterizes it as the start of a new Cold War. Want to

South Africa and a Return to Civilization 147

put a bomb in a U.S. city? Put it in a 40-foot sailboat and sail it into a harbor. No one would catch it.

The U.S. is not concerned about the environment, but the rest of the developed world is. Perhaps the relevant treaties are flawed, but just to back out is seen here as typically "American." Because we use such a disproportionate share of the world's resources, we should at least fully participate in their management.

Then there's the Test Ban Treaty. As I write, Bush is traveling in Europe and getting some shit. Well-deserved, it seems to me.

I hope I don't lose readership because of what I've just said; but I feel better for having said it. Now I'll go back to reporting.—Bob

I considered pruning the above, but feel just as strongly about these issues now as I did then. My extensive exposure to other people and other countries has sensitized me to how others feel about many things, including the U.S. We are loved and admired for our popular music, blue jeans, technology, and much more. We are loathed for being a bully. And it's important.

27

Touring Africa: Wildlife and People

After her two months high and dry, *Chandelle* carried me gracefully back to the dock in Durban. She glowed with new paint inside and out, and when it rained, her deck no longer leaked. She was ready for more sea-time, but I had another adventure in mind. Friends Sue and Joanne from Boston had set up a safari in Kenya and had urged me to go along. I had to get the boat-work done first and I made it just in time. I dropped into a travel agent's office two blocks from the dock to find the agent sweeping broken glass off her desk. In response to my question, she pointed to a hole in the window above the desk—a bullet hole. Then I remembered hearing firecracker sounds the evening before. Police had cornered car thieves and the ensuing confrontation took out the agent's window. Just another day in Durban, South Africa.

The agent, nonchalant, handed me the tickets. Here is the email I wrote on my return.

> October 20, 2001—Greetings Everyone.
>
> I am now back from my safari, and the boat is still afloat here in Durban. Words and photography cannot do justice to my experience in Kenya. The vistas, the animal herds, the visits to native villages, the sounds of lions near our tents at night are beyond my ability to describe. I attempt it for those who have made a similar trip and want to compare and for anyone contemplating such a trip. I have had unusual experiences over the last several years, and Kenya ranks near the top.
>
> My plane from Durban flew right by Mt. Kilimanjaro—quite a sight. In October (late spring) there was still snow on top. Our guide, Clive, met me at the airport. Six-foot-five and 250 pounds, he was a bigger-than-life character. An ex-rugby player and former U.K. Army (Special Services), he took part in every military operation during his 22 years of service. He had extensive

knowledge of the animals, birds, and natives of Kenya, and his 10 years there gave him contacts and insights beyond those of the average guide.

Joined by Sue and Joanne, we did tourist things around Nairobi, the best of which was a visit to an elephant orphanage. The fascinating woman who runs it has been successful in returning approximately 30 animals to the wild using a process too complicated to go into here. She is now working on three young ones. We were "introduced" and played with the youngest. To say hello to an elephant you grab its trunk and breathe into it so it knows you. The youngster would reward us by trying to knock us over, then stand back and look amused.

Next day we boarded Clive's Land Rover and drove to the Aberdare National Park and The Ark. You may have heard of Treetops, the lodge where many famous people have stayed (including my parents, 42 years ago, and the Queen of England). Tragically, the park has been denuded near Treetops, and The Ark, located nearer the park's center, now provides the best animal watching—from a five-star hotel that is. The Ark is built in the forest right by a watering hole and in such a way that one can view animals while sitting inside by a fire or on a balcony or in a "hide." The food was excellent and the towels so thick and fuzzy, I couldn't get even one into my duffel.

Animal watching is The Ark's *raison d'être*. We saw animals and birds too numerous to count. Because the animals were likely to show up in the middle of the night, when one did, the hotel staff rang a bell: one ring for a zebra, two for an elephant, three for a lion. If at 2:00 a.m., you heard two bells, you could say to yourself, "I've seen elephants," and go back to sleep.

Next day we drove to the Samburu National Reserve and stayed at the Intrepid Safari camp, more a hotel than a camp. With that as a base, we went on game drives every morning and evening and visited a Samburu village. Clive knew this village well, and all the available "warriors" and ladies performed several dances just for us, all in full costume. They dress in full costume all the time, with robes almost exclusively in red, similar to the Masai, whom we met later. Few in this village were literate, although two or three spoke a few words of English. There was a school for the younger ones. We were in the area three days.

Next we drove to the well-known Masai Mara National Reserve, where Clive's gang (there were seven for the three of us) had set up camp. What a rough camp it was. Each day at 6:00 a.m.—it's sunrise and sunset when the good stuff happens—a gentle voice by the tent flap said, "Good morning," as the owner of the voice poured heated water into a washbowl. A quick cup of coffee and we were off by Land Rover. As the sun rose, often dramatically, we saw gazelles, elephants, lions, cheetahs, buffalo, and more all in their natural state (which might mean eating each other). Then back to camp for a hearty breakfast, cooked by Clemant. I don't know how or where he learned to cook, but he was good and his bread was superb.

After breakfast, with Clive toting a large field piece in case we were attacked by a lion or rhino, we might take a short hike or visit a Masai village.

The Masai wore colorful dress, although not in our honor. They always wore their red robes and many beads. Back at camp, Clive's gang, having moved the table from a tent to the side of a nearby stream, served us lunch. Later, an evening game drive was followed by a hot shower, followed by another great meal by Clemant. Attempts at meaningful conversation after dinner were useless; we regularly crashed.

We saw animals and birds, gorgeous vistas, beautiful sunrises and sunsets. On walks we had a Masai guide who was phenomenal at spotting game. He showed us tracks in the dirt and the difference between zebra, wildebeest, ostrich, and adidas. High points include watching a cheetah chase a herd of Thompson's gazelles all going flat out for 200 yards (the cheetah went hungry that night) and watching a buffalo suddenly chase a lion. Clive said he had never seen that in all his years there. Lions usually eat the buffalo. A big male elephant suddenly took a dislike to us and *charged*. I have a sequence of pictures of him, the last blurred by dust as Clive put the hammer down on the Land Rover to get us out of there.

We also visited a Masai school. It was more impressive than the one we'd visited in the Samburu. Tragically, female circumcision (a misnomer if ever there was one) is still practiced in these villages. The practice is dying, we are assured; however, the decision is made not by the girl but by village elders or parents. There seemed no way to impart our influence. We were so warmly welcomed by these kind, gentle people that to raise such a topic would have been totally out of place.

We could easily have spent a month at the camp, with (of course) Clive's gang doing the cooking, cleanup, wood-gathering, bed-making, washing, etc. We left with memories to last a lifetime. Africa is not what it was, but it is better than it will be. The time to visit is now.

For those not interested in my worldview (there are many), please skip to the end. For the rest of you, yes, I've had help or feedback in my role here as U.S. representative on the dock. I appreciate it. Certainly the U.S. does more things right than most other countries, but we look so arrogant by the manner in which we cancel treaties and protocols. One can find scientists on any part of the environmental spectrum one wants, but their predominant view is that global warming is cause for concern. I cite recent issues of *Time Magazine* and *Scientific American* on this topic. Because of pursuing our missile-defense shield, the Russians have already threatened to stop reducing their nuclear arsenal and threatened to sell nuclear technology to the Chinese, who are angry at us for selling arms to Taiwan. Will India and Pakistan be far behind in developing their own bomb? A newspaper here asks if this is the start of another Cold War. I fail to see how our actions promote a safer world for anyone. To borrow a phrase from Vince Lombardi, "Making friends isn't everything, but making enemies isn't anything."

OK, I'll stop. I have lots of things to do here, trips to take, always boat work, etc.—Bob

After Kenya, it was tough getting back to the real world of Durban and the boat. The boat always reminded me of projects, and Clive and his gang were not available to help. Firecrackers in Durban again turned out to be gunfire, but I'd already begun planning my next step. Now that I'd seen something of central Africa, I wanted to see southern Africa or South Africa itself. Here's the email I sent from Cape Town.

January 15, 2002—Greetings from Cape Town, South Africa.
Time to bring you up to date on the wanderings of *Chandelle* and her captain. On returning from Kenya, I fell into the routine of boat projects and side events. My friends down the dock and I went on local trips, to concerts to see our friends in the symphony perform, to parties with these musicians, and to plays. Mostly because of the people involved, but also because I never stopped one of the bullets that occasionally zinged around town, I will always remember fondly my stay in Durban.
Still, there was more to see. With Judy Orlando, a dear friend from home, I traveled to game parks, including Kruger, South Africa's most famous national park. Great stuff. However, I had made the mistake of going to Kenya first. Kenya was hard to top.
I joined a tour to Botswana and Victoria Falls and flew up to Maun, Botswana, to meet the group. Except for the guide, I was the only one over 30. He acted 25 much of the time, but did his job and we got along fine. First leg was to the Okavango Delta. Like the Florida Everglades, the Delta has vast areas of slowly moving water. It is host to many unusual species and to herds of large animals. We took a two-hour plane trip and saw herds larger than any in Kenya. Once on the ground we saw few herds because the vegetation was high and dense. We had to be content with sleeping under the stars and letting the natives paddle us around in their dugout canoes.
Next up was a drive in the tour bus to Chobe Game Park on the eastern edge of Botswana. It was dry and fiercely hot—over 100°F. Every half-hour or so we saw the carcass of a horse or cow that had succumbed to the heat and would soon be food for vultures. Chobe has fewer varieties of animals than Kenya, but is an elephant hunter's paradise. The pachyderm population was out of control and vegetation suffered. Botswana used to cull elephants. Under pressure from various groups, it is now trying to transfer elephants to other parks—an expensive and dangerous task. A recent issue of *National Geographic* discusses an effort to extend and combine several parks. Although that would be great for the animals, it would present huge political hurdles for the natives and countries involved.
After a hot and dry half-day's drive, we arrived at Victoria Falls. We went to the Zambian side because it was cheaper and easier to get fuel. Zimbabwe is out of fuel and out of responsible government. The falls are indeed spectacular: lots of water falling a long way. The chasm is part of the Great African

Rift, a fissure in the earth stretching from near the Mediterranean almost to Madagascar. In Kenya we had crossed it more than once.

My trip was marred by three events. I left Durban with a toothache, a worry for two or three days, and left Vic Falls with stomach flu. Worst was that the trip followed by four days the events of September 11, 2001. I was the only American around and there was nothing I could do. I called several people back home. That likely helped me more than it helped them. Friends here were all supportive, but I found sleep difficult for several days.

I have been asked to comment on support for the U.S. here. Mostly, we have support. While local Muslim leaders staged anti-U.S. rallies, they were not well-attended. I saw one a few blocks away in Durban that attracted perhaps 200 people. They made a lot of noise, but no one near me paid any attention. I declined to get involved. I had one chat in a coffee shop with a chap who turned out to be a police investigator. A Muslim, I asked him what the U.S. should do. He reflected a minute and said, "You have to bomb them."

Referring to September 11, a local newspaper used the word *atrocities*, when it could have used *events*. I live with a paucity of detail, but as I write, things seem to be going better than expected. All my fingers and toes are crossed. As I've said before, we are vilified when we do something dumb and often when we don't; but we are also admired. Right now support seems strong.

However, I digress.

Looming—threatening—in my future for a long time has been the sail from Durban to Cape Town. The weather can be fierce. Gales are common and the Aguilas Current flows up to 5 knots. When the gales oppose the current, waves as high as 50 and 75 feet have destroyed commercial shipping. *Chandelle* would not be happy in such conditions; neither would her skipper.

Delivering boats along this coast is a business. I decided to hire an experienced hand. I was introduced to a former businessman with a master's degree in accounting. I had been warned not to judge him by his appearance. Short and slim, with lots of hair confined to his neck and beard, he was a First World drop-out who looked like a semi-reformed addict. However, he had made the trip over eight times. He turned out to be charming and just what I was looking for. He brought along his wife and a young man whom I hoped would stay with me all the way home to New York.

We four headed into the unknown. The wind was forecast to be behind us and it was. For the first two days, it brought torrential rain. We were soaked, as was the boat. Finally, the rain stopped, but the wind did not. Wind and current were both going our way. We stayed in the current and flew. Wind was in the 40-knot range with one gust to 56 knots. We were doing 8-9 knots through the water, and with the current, often 11 knots over the bottom. In one 24-hour period we clocked 230 nautical miles, surpassing *Chandelle*'s earlier record of 179 miles.

Most boats have to stop along the way to hide from weather, and trips can take up to three weeks. We made it in four days, eight hours, which we thought a record. I mentioned this at the bar in the Royal Cape Yacht Club. Not to be outdone, a South African, a few stools away, said he had done it in three days, 18 hours. He was six-foot-four, well over 200 pounds, and fortified with a number of beers. I didn't challenge him.

Cape Town is gorgeous, although as I write it is blowing 40 knots and I'm regularly checking the docking lines. I've been to town a few times and it is cleaner, more prosperous, and safer than Durban. I will miss my Durban friends, but such is this life. Soon I fly back to Durban to pick up my car, and with friend Bill Winters, drive the Garden Route—reportedly superb—before returning to Cape Town. From here I'll sail to the Caribbean, arriving maybe in March, then sail on home.

Since I am coming to the end of my African visit, I feel a need to comment. Although I've experienced only a small portion of the continent, that won't stop me. I see no way that the black-European conflict in South Africa could have been avoided. Lessened, yes, but not avoided. The societies are too different. The Europeans brought farming and ultimately technology. Many of the natives' habits and belief systems make assimilation into the First World difficult. What has impressed me here is the difficulty of changing the beliefs, habits, and mindsets impeding assimilation. Do you recall my relating the corn-growing event with my farming friend? (The white farmer's quality seeds grew well, but the black recipients were threatened by neighbors whose corn grew less well.) Massive education, for which there wasn't the will nor now the money, is the right course, but it will take generations of dedication to make the changes necessary to bring about a high-tech society.

Why have a high-tech society? It might be wonderful for all those who are frustrated and desperately underemployed to go back to subsistence farming, but there are too many of them. The only way so many can eat is to have efficient farming and the society to go along with it. Look at Zimbabwe. White farmers are being driven off, replaced by hordes of natives who will be lucky to feed themselves. Those in the city will be hungry. The papers here are predicting a humanitarian crisis. Would things be different, if 40 years ago, those in the South African government had pushed for education instead of apartheid? Yes, but they didn't. Animosity over apartheid contributes to the high rate of crime and corruption.

In Kenya there is massive poverty and substantial crime and corruption, yet at a rugby game I attended, there was much jocularity between blacks and whites. I mentioned this to my host, who knew South Africa. He said that in Kenya there was far less tension. In South Africa, blacks play and watch soccer, whites play and watch rugby and cricket; there is no mixing.

Botswana and Namibia have been held up to me as paragons of good, black government. Perhaps. We visited a school in Botswana that had sturdy buildings and well-fed students in good-looking uniforms. However, Botswana has the highest HIV/AIDS rate in Africa. How effective is their education? That leaves Namibia. I'm told there are other African countries doing well. I haven't found them.

Most deaths occur from non-AIDS diseases and are more easily preventable with better hygiene and clean water. Is it cruel to say that a major effort toward AIDS prevention would aggravate the already disastrous population problem? AIDS can be prevented by changing individual behavior. Men here won't change. You are not a man unless you have sex with many women regularly. At a local university the male students recently demanded, and presumably got, unlimited access to the women's dorms. "Our rules now," said the black students. On marches AIDS. The official government position is that HIV does not lead to AIDS. It would take huge amounts of effort and money to treat the tragedy meaningfully. It is hard to avoid words like *hopeless* when thinking of the African continent.

After sailing to Cape Town, I flew back to Durban to pick up my car and U.S. friend Bill. We drove down the east coast, justly called the Garden Route. The coast alternates between beach and forest. The roads are mostly excellent; the bed-and-breakfasts and farm-stays, wonderful. South Africa recognizes the potential bonanza of tourism and has invested in the industry. We stayed in towns like Kokstad, East London, Addo, Storms River, and Knysna, then went north to the Karoo, a large area of rocky mountains, desert, and luxurious farms. We stayed one night in Prince Albert, where we met a former Cambridge classmate of Bill Clinton's (the class was surprised he did so well), then on to Oudtshoorn, Barrydale, and Montague. This last is near a town called Ashton—a seedy town, but with a winery by that name. I bought a case. These towns were often separated by mountains, and dramatic passes had been carved for the roads. One, called the Swartberg Pass in honor of the designing engineer (engineers get too few honors), is maintained in a primitive state by law. Only marginally navigable by my '90 Honda, it was particularly stunning.

We made a short stop in Cape Town to see if the boat was still afloat. It was, so we headed north to such places as Cederberg, Tulbagh, and Ceres. This area was even more dramatic, with steep, rocky mountains and valleys filled with vineyards, citrus trees, and farms. We toured wineries and ostrich farms. Ostriches are raised here for both feathers and meat—the meat is especially tasty. We also watched a parasailing meet. Folks with parachute-like devices step off a hillside to be carried on the wind. While these devices are not as effective as sailplanes or hang gliders, they are more convenient. At the end of the day, parasailers fold up their toys to the size of a large backpack and go home. We went on wonderful hikes in magnificent country and met interesting people all along the way.

I took many tours in and around Cape Town, including the Cape of Good Hope, the Botanical Gardens, and the Victoria and Albert Waterfront. A particularly memorable day was the combination tour of Robbin Island and a black township. Robbin Island was where many black activists were imprisoned, including Nelson Mandela for 27 years. The tour was conducted by a one-time prisoner. We were shown the black township where most blacks in Cape Town live by a resident who pointed out the levels of housing within the township, from cardboard-and-tin shacks to concrete-block dwellings to houses with lawns and flowers and TV dish antennas. The houses were owned by doctors, lawyers, and other professionals who had made it and who chose to stay in the township. Welcome role models.

People who consider visiting South Africa hear mostly about AIDS and crime. South Africa deserves a better reputation. First, AIDS is a non-issue for the visitor unless you go looking for it. Second, crime is avoidable. Behave as you would in any big city and there is little problem. There are horror stories, yes. My car went wandering (was stolen) a couple of times, but that can happen anywhere. As I write, a dollar is worth 12 rand. When Bill and I were traveling, nowhere did dinner, bed, and breakfast cost us more than $25. For anyone on a budget, this place is a gem. And there is a lot to do; I've just scratched the surface. At a delightful dinner party I attended last night (it was Christmas), there was a lady about to retire from the U.K. Foreign Service. She had lived almost everywhere and was seriously considering retiring to Cape Town.

After gathering crew, *Chandelle* will leave for the last legs of the journey home. I'm seriously conflicted. I'm looking forward to being home, but not sure I want the trip to end. It will be interesting to see how this conflict resolves.

Enough for now. It is holiday season and I wish everyone the best for 2002. May it be free of horrors.—Warm regards to all, Bob

There was a lot of water ahead—6,000 miles to New York. I felt the usual apprehension. Now, near the end of the trip, the possibility of a catastrophe troubled me more than it had in the beginning. I knew more of what could go wrong. Wanting to be well-prepared, I'd made a substantial investment in boat maintenance and had even replaced the life raft. For one more trip, the old one probably would have been OK, but the new, high-tech one was lighter, easier to store, and easier to deploy. It was also expensive, in part because its compressed-air tank required flying it to South Africa under a special category. After the crossing, I counted on selling it and recouping most of my cost.

A small voice was telling me that an era was about to close. Most of the land adventure was over. The islands of the South Pacific, the mountains of New Zealand, the elephants of Kenya were behind me. The sea ahead held both fascination and danger. I consider myself a sailor, but I didn't do all this just to sail; I did it to see the world. I had seen most of what I had come for; yet I wasn't entirely happy that the adventure was coming to an end.

28

Going Home—at Last

Loaded with crew, bread, eggs, beer, and a thousand other things, *Chandelle* headed to sea. My email, written in St Lucia, tells the story.

March 25, 2002—Greetings to All from St. Lucia, Eastern Caribbean.

By arrival here, on March 21, *Chandelle* and her captain completed the circumnavigation. *Chandelle* was last here on June 10, 1994.

The trip started with the arrival in Cape Town of long-time friend Jon Stoddard, who had sailed with me on two previous trips, and surprisingly, wanted to go again. Thank goodness he did; he was an enormous help. He arrived two weeks early and we sampled Cape Town, the wine country, and the wine. Jon had just climbed Kilimanjaro, an impressive feat. During the Cape Town touring, we planned for the passage. I had signed on the young man I had met in Durban, who sailed to Cape Town with me and had agreed to go all the way to New York. However, when it came time for him to buy a return ticket, he bailed out.

Notices went back on bulletin boards and we wound up with Jacques Nothling, a 31-year-old South African who was a character. He had plenty of sailing experience, was willing, strong as an ox, and had a great, though ribald, sense of humor. To our surprise, he was also an excellent cook.

Having made major investments in the boat in South Africa, I was confident of a reasonably trouble-free trip. Neptune had other plans. Shortly after leaving the harbor, the starter battery died, which meant starting the diesel with house batteries. Then the head picked up trash and became difficult to operate. There was more.

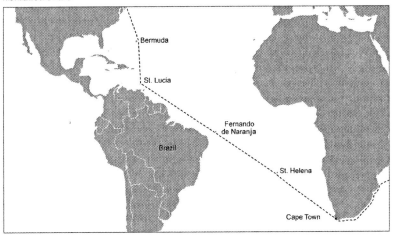

The Atlantic and Home

After provisioning, stowing, and last-minute fixing, we backed out of the dock at the Royal Cape Yacht Club on 02/02/2002. What date could be luckier? Many boats are built in South Africa for sale to owners in the U.S. and the Caribbean and are delivered by sailing them there. We had talked to delivery skippers about best routes: Great Circle? Rhumb line? North of the rhumb? They all had different ideas. Figuring there was no magic route, we let optimum wind angle determine our course. Winds were light in the harbor and though I hated to use fuel at the beginning, we motored for the first few hours. Soon a good wind came up—light, but sufficient. Light winds became the hallmark of the trip and were always behind us. We used every sail combination we could think of, along with motoring now and then, and arrived in St. Helena on February 13.

St. Helena is a rocky island right in the middle of the South Atlantic. Not the best harbor, yet a welcome breather in a long trip. Yes, it's where Napoleon was imprisoned and finally died. The weather was rainy, so we didn't tour much. We ate mediocre meals ashore, wandered around town, and climbed nearby Jacobs Ladder—900 steps up a steep hill. Even the aging captain made it.

We topped off fuel and provisions, and on February 17, pulled the anchor and headed north. The next goal was Fernando de Naranja, a small island near the easternmost point of Brazil. The weather was similar to the prior leg but with the advantage, at least part of the time, of a favorable current. Part of the time it was also hot. During the day we cowered under extra shades, draped a white sheet over the dark-green bimini, drank lots of water, and occasionally dumped buckets of seawater on ourselves. We had many days of spectacular, care-free sailing: wind behind and steady, sail combinations working well, seas not severe enough to hinder the cooks. They did a great job. So did the dishwasher (me). We arrived on March 1.

Fernando was frustrating. Almost no one spoke English. There were no banks that could change money. Few establishments would take credit cards. We had tried to get local currency in Cape Town to no avail. We ate two good meals ashore and rented a car for a day. Known for scuba diving, the island is probably an excellent place, if you speak Portuguese. We tried snorkeling, but it had just rained heavily and waters were cloudy.

After doing what provisioning we could (there wasn't much available) and topping off with fuel, we tried to depart. The anchor chain had snagged on the bottom and no matter what we did—yanking this way, then that—we couldn't get it loose. I pulled myself down the chain as far as my lungs would permit, but couldn't see anything, much less do anything about the snag.

Fortunately, we were in a dive center. However, everyone was either busy or didn't speak English or both. Finally I located two teenagers willing to help. They came out in a small boat and had tanks, but no regulator. One took a tank in his arms and disappeared underwater. We followed him by watching bubbles rising along the anchor chain as he pulled himself down while holding onto the tank and getting air by opening the valve directly. I don't know how he did it. One hand to follow the chain, one arm to grasp the tank—how could he also open the air valve and clear the snag? In five minutes he surfaced wearing a big grin. "It's OK now," he said, and it was. They got a big tip. Finally, at 2:00 p.m. on March 6, we were underway.

This would not be an easy leg. Not enough wind in the beginning meant motoring: using fuel when we least wanted to. We had expected to meet the doldrums on this passage and we met them right away. We had little wind, torrential rains, and a significant current (1-1.5 knots) against us. Such a current may not seem like much, but it has a big effect. You can't stop and wait for a breeze; you have to get out of the area. You can't run at a slow speed to save fuel because the current destroys efficiency. Some of the time we had wind on the nose and had to tack. You don't make much progress sailing 50° off course, doing 4.5 knots through the water with 1.5 knots against you.

Taking inventory, we found we had used two-thirds of our fuel traveling one-quarter of the distance to our goal. What could we do? We talked about turning off the fridge or hand-steering. We had food for all circumstances. We would not go hungry. Still, we had a big investment in frozen and refrigerated food; losing it was not an attractive proposition. We had an opposing current for five or six days. None of the delivery skippers we talked to had mentioned anything like this. The current situation slowly improved, yet favorable winds alternated with calm spells. Our circumstances were already bad enough when the main halyard parted and the mainsail slid down the mast. We had no spare main halyard and no other way to support the main. As I write, it appears that the rigger in Durban got the halyard or halyards crossed. Was it crossed with the jib halyard—also a cable? Was that about to go?

The jib halyard did not part and winds improved. We were about 6°North at the time, having struggled up from 3°South at Fernando. We ran the engine only for battery-charging and raised the fridge temperature, trusting the Cryovac process to preserve our meats. (It did.)

For the last several days, we had good winds and the jib alone drove us at 6-7 knots. The final morning heading to St. Lucia was breezy, bright, and sunny. We saw the island of Barbados about 90 miles off, and late in the day, watched a spectacular sunset over St. Lucia, while sipping wine in the cockpit before a fine dinner on deck. Even with its trials, this life is worth it.

We entered Rodney Bay at about 10:00 p.m. I don't like night landings, but I'd been here before: June 10th, 1994, to be exact. Now it was March 21, 2002. We snuggled up near two megayachts, dropped the hook, took a celebratory sip of rum, and went to sleep. We were all happy and glad to be here. I had the added joy of having sailed around the world.

Still two legs to go: St. Lucia to Bermuda, Bermuda to New York. I plan to stay here for awhile. I'm not home, but I feel more relaxed. I know support services are here and any problem can be solved. It should be easy from here on. We'll see.—Bob

Old Neptune hadn't forgotten me. The following email tells the story.

June 3, 2002—Dear Family and Friends: Greetings from New York.

Yes, *Chandelle* and crew arrived safely a few days ago, and she is tied up in City Island. Home port.

My last major communication was from St. Lucia in the Caribbean where we completed the circumnavigation. The challenges and pleasures were not over.

To rest and wait for optimum weather, I planned to spend time in St. Lucia. I hadn't toured it before and persuaded good friend Lucy Kirk to join me. On returning from a day tour, I found a note from South African crewman Jacques Nothling, who had sailed with Jon and me from Cape Town. He had had "an emergency at home" and "had to take the next flight out." Jon had left days earlier according to plan. There was no further explanation from Jacques nor any subsequent communication. He'd obviously had a better job offer and had taken it. He had promised to go all the way to New York and that was the basis for my taking him on. He was well aware of my need, and I was more than a little upset with him.

Once more, I needed crew. There seemed to be a dearth of crew in St. Lucia so I decided to go to Antigua, where the annual Race Week was about to begin. Single-handing can be satisfying (some do a circumnavigation that way) and the challenge of single-handing to Antigua had momentary appeal. However, boat problems made the trip potentially difficult, such as finding a rigger to replace the main halyard. When Lucy suggested that she go along, I was delighted. Her help was key on several occasions. We had good days, but on rough days, Lucy would ask me if this was a fun day, and I would confess that it was not.

Expecting to find more beach hotels, bigger crowds, and more crime than when I was here eight years ago, I had planned to visit the Caribbean only minimally. I was pleasantly surprised. There were new hotels, yet the crowds didn't seem any bigger and crime was down. At the urging of local governments, police are particularly hard on crime against tourists. The place is beautiful, and when you can wait for weather, the sailing is terrific.

Eventually, we pulled into English Harbor on Antigua. It's a great harbor and yachting center and a museum piece from the days of the square-riggers. When we arrived, the harbor was buzzing with crews readying boats for racing or partying. I had heard that Race Week was a swinging time. I quote the poet Norman Levy:

> But I, though warned and fortified,
> Was deeply shocked and mortified,
> To find on my arrival wild debauchery in sway.
> While some lay in a stupor sent,
> By booze of more than two percent,
> The others were behaving in a *most* immoral way.

Folks were having a great time.

Lucy departed for the normal life in New York, and I began my search for crew. There are actually two race weeks. The first is "Classic Week" for old boats, not-so-old boats, and new boats built along classic lines. All are polished and buffed to compete for looks without reference to sailing. There were two J-boats, *Valshida* and *Shamrock V*, both about 125 feet; at least two boats bigger than they; and many more boats in the 75- to 100-foot range. All were gleaming in the sun.

I developed a desperate need to see them in action and went looking for an observation boat. Someone suggested I talk to "that woman over there." She was a delightful lady, who had arranged with a local charity to sell spaces on the competitors in exchange for a contribution. It was a hefty contribution, but to a good charity, and it got one on one of the competing boats. I couldn't believe my luck. She suggested a boat for me and it was perfect. It was a new boat built by father and son along classic lines. I have seen many home-built boats in my travels; none compared to the quality of this one. They were wonderful people: the father and son, the son's girlfriend, and another man who had been a major contributor to the building project. I was welcomed—especially when I told them I'd done lots of sailing and some racing. They had not sailed much and had never raced.

We had a great time and perhaps I was able to help them. The design they built, while handsome, didn't sail well. We were not competitive, but among the rewards was just being in the race. As is often done, the fastest boats were started last and had to sail through the rest of us. The thrill of seeing a J rushing by on one side about 30 feet away and a bigger one rushing by on the other side about 20 feet away, will be with me for a long time. I took pictures, but was hampered by also needing to be both grinder and tactician.

One evening I roamed into a local bar (not my habit) and saw among the usual 25-year-old mainstays, a handsome older couple. I struck up a conversation and learned that they were on the Race Committee for the non-classic Race Week coming up next. I promptly volunteered to help anyway I could, expecting to hand out flyers or answer questions at the desk. To my astonishment, the next day they came by my boat and offered me the job of gunner on the committee boat. I accepted instantly.

Each race day (there were five), I rose early, climbed on the 55-foot catamaran chartered by the committee; ate breakfast snacks; drank all the soft drinks, beer, and wine I wanted; and consumed the catered lunch (the lobster salad was to die for). All I had to do was fire the gun at the right moments. That took concentration, but I got it about right. The gun was a shotgun and even the blanks were loud. The chief thrill for me was watching the starts. Having raced myself, I was fascinated to watch professional skippers, whose jobs depended on doing well, drive these multi-million-dollar toys and jockey for position at close range and top speed. This was world-class sailing. More than one shouting match ensued, but no collisions.

During Race Week, I neglected my reason for being there: to find crew. Five years ago I was in the Fiji Islands and had missed my 50th high school reunion. Now there was the 55th, and I wanted to make this one. Several classmates had urged me to attend, and I'd been scheduled as the speaker for lunch. I had figured previously that I would be in Bermuda and had made a plane reservation on that assumption. Now I had to get to Bermuda. I could do it, if I sailed right after Race Week. However, I was on the committee boat all day and crew wasn't finding me.

I met a local man who ran a help facility for yachts and explained my plight. He recommended a native, Anderson Jackson. I would have to pay him a good sum (the first time I'd done that, except for rounding the Cape of Good Hope), but I had little choice. I was all set to go with the two of us when a young American, Wade Roberts, expressed interest. Anderson didn't have a U.S. visa and couldn't go on to the U.S. Also, he would cost me while he watched my boat in Bermuda. So I took on Wade as well. I paid him, too, but less.

The three of us sailed to Bermuda. We had a good trip—six days with mostly trade winds on the beam—though we motored most of the last day. Anderson was a superb sailor. Agile and strong, he had a flair for sail trim. Wade was less experienced but was a good cook. Since I was paying them, I made them take the night watch. I'd done enough night watches. During the day, while crew slept, I could sail the boat as I wanted to. I got used to that quickly.

Everyone got along well, and as soon as we reached Bermuda, the young folks went out on the town. Wade took pride in his ability to party. He wasn't happy unless he was hung-over, yet he did a fine job for me. Anderson was quiet when with us, but I heard later that he'd got himself in a lot of trouble back in Antigua.

In Bermuda, we tied up to the wall in St. George. I put Anderson on a plane back to Antigua, left Wade in charge of *Chandelle*, and flew to my reunion. The reunion was great. I'm glad I took the trouble. We were a small class, and therefore, close. Several members of the football and soccer teams kidded each other about who had dropped this pass or missed that block. I talked about my trip at lunch, but with only a world map and no pictures or slides, the talk must have been boring.

As the plane approached Bermuda on the trip back, the pilot came on the intercom and reported 35-knot winds from the south. I winced. That's the worst kind of wind for a boat on the wall in St. George. What had Wade done? I was frantic to see the instant we landed. However, I had no return plane ticket. That's a no-no in Bermuda. I had to see a special Immigration officer at the airport for permission to enter. There was a line. Although it seemed like hours, it was likely only a half-hour before I could get to the officer and explain my status. He was sympathetic and stamped my passport. I dashed to the taxi line. As we wound around the island, I watched trees bending over in the wind. Finally, turning the corner by the harbor, I saw to my great relief, *Chandelle* bouncing away, padded with the extra fenders Wade had borrowed from other boats. All was well.

For the trip home, I wanted one more crew. I had asked Wade to be on the lookout while I was away, and he introduced me to Brandon Hall, a slim young man of about 30 from the Deep South. He said he had done a lot of sailing and seemed to know his way around boats, so I signed him up. I was now stuck with having to pay him, too.

The boat and the three of us were ready to go, but the weather was squally and rainy and not what Bermudans like to brag about. One forecaster gave a short window from late one day to noon the next. We were not provisioned to leave that moment, and early the next day, the weather was awful. When it let up somewhat, Wade and Brandon wanted to go. I was pretty sure that if we did not go, we'd wait a week for better weather and they would fly out, leaving me with no crew at all. So we scrambled for provisions and prepared for a rough trip. While I was doing the paperwork with Customs, the crew from another boat was checking in. They had headed out a couple of hours earlier and their mast had broken. That added to my considerable apprehension. We went anyway.

The next 24 hours were perhaps the worst of my nearly 10-year trip. Once we had rounded the reefs and were committed, the winds picked up to 40-45 knots on the beam. I had expected a broad reach, which would have been much more comfortable. Not to be. All too often, we had breaking seas hitting us broadside. I was seasick for the first time in my life. Not once, but twice. So was Wade. Waves were breaking regularly on the cabin top. I was happy I had been completely re-rigged in South Africa. The strain on the rigging was tremendous. Things calmed down after 24 hours, and we all felt better.

For the next several days we had light winds and spent part of the time motoring. It was slow, yet relatively pleasant. The Gulf Stream, known for heavy weather, was unusually flat.

Reaching New York Harbor, we ran into heavy fog—only the second time I'd sailed in fog in over 10 years. It was midday. The tide charts showed the current against us in the East River. The diesel could never overcome the current, so we went into Sandy Hook to wait for the following day. On the way in through a channel that hardly ever has traffic, I listened to the cacophony of fog horns and suddenly recognized four toots: collision course. Surely not us. I glanced at the radar. Returns everywhere. Hard to sort out. Four more toots. Closer. It *was* us. I did a 90° turn out of the channel as a huge freighter loomed out of the fog. Way too close for comfort and a lesson learned. Pay attention. A channel seldom used can still have hazards.

We picked up a mooring in Great Kills on Staten Island and celebrated with a drink in the cockpit. Then, early the next day, we ran New York harbor on a spring tide, reaching 10 knots on GPS in the East River. It's best to do the East River on slack tide, but after sailing all the way around the world, I didn't want to wait. Next time, I'll wait. Eddy currents were so strong, Harvey couldn't handle the steering. We almost hit shore a couple of times. That would have been an unfitting finale. I steered by hand. Finally, about noon, we reached Minnefords Yacht Yard on City Island and tied up for the last time this trip. It was May 28, 2002.

Home at Last

Many thoughts crowd in. I'm excited to be home. I'll miss many aspects of the cruising life. Not all, but many. The two most difficult things have been being away from family and close friends and needing regularly to find crew. I have been extremely lucky in never having bad crew on the trip. Most have been wonderful. I am in touch with many by email. (They number close to 20.) There were differences in age or philosophy and there were other commitments, of course, but I am profoundly grateful to all for making the trip possible. The challenge of dealing with age and other differences was as much theirs as mine.

What have I learned during these nearly 10 years? Boat maintenance. Geography. That there are many wonderful people in the world. That having a country like the U.S. to come home to is an extraordinary good fortune. That most people around the world have a tough life. Lots more. And oh yes—reef early.

Because my apartment is still rented, I am living on the boat this summer. I expect to enjoy it. I plan lots of trips, more by car than by boat. (I've done a lot of sailing recently.) I have projects. There is always something to do on the boat.

What then? I don't know. We'll all have to wait and see.—Bob

With a cell phone and a car, living on the boat at City Island was perfectly easy. It was easy to get into the city and easy to see friends in Connecticut. Looking back, I was surprised that I went for a sail only once, and then to take friends who had been unusually kind to me. Yes, I had done a lot of sailing. Looking out from my dock, the waters of Long Island Sound didn't call to me as the waters of Polynesia had.

I had always thought that I'd keep the boat for a year or so and make a slow transition to city life, but I didn't use it. About the time I started to face the bills for winter storage, I got an offer for *Chandelle* from a young man I had met in Antigua. It was an emotional day when I made the decision to sell. It seemed disloyal, like abandoning a dear friend. But the buyers, a young couple, were talking of sailing around the world. *Chandelle* would like that. Made the decision easier.

There is a tragic end. The couple sailed the boat to Antigua (in the middle of winter) but found they had a problem: they didn't get along. He left; she lived on board for a few months. Mysteriously, the boat was "stolen" from its berth in English Harbor. It caught fire and sank a few yards from the harbor entrance. Yes, it's sad, but *Chandelle* had a good life. She saw more of the world than most of her kin. I normally avoid anthropomorphic comparisons, but she rests now in a medium she knows, perhaps with a smile of satisfaction on her prow.

My satisfaction is similar. The phrase "trip of a lifetime" is over-used, but it was that and more. Its effect on me (beyond the challenge to talk about something else) is likely more substantial than I know. The challenges met cover the spectrum—mechanical, emotional, and physical. I don't deny the satisfaction, but I would be remiss not to credit an awesome amount of luck: surviving a storm in Sag Harbor two weeks after I bought her when most of the other boats were destroyed (I didn't mention this earlier because it occurred before the big trip); her anchors dragging when someone happened to be watching; the boy on the beach in Indonesia whose diligence provided rescue after *Chandelle* had dragged over a mile to sea; being stuck on a reef in Fiji and sustaining only minor damage; lightning striking other boats, but not us; gear failure when it was not life-threatening; and not least, phenomenal luck with crew.

Save for four short trips home, I was away for nine-and-a-half years, missing family, friends, movies, parties, and all the safety and comfort of the U.S.A. Have I any regrets? Not one. Not one.

978-0-595-38903-2
0-595-38903-1

Printed in the United States
59512LVS00003B/169-561